~ THE ~

WINE

L A B E L
Collector's

• A L B U M •

NED HALLEY

~ THE ~

WINE

LABEL

Collector's

ALBUM

NED HALLEY

LITTLE, BROWN & COMPANY
Boston • Toronto • London

First edition

ISBN 0-316-88875-3
A CIP catalogue record for this book
is available from the British Library

Designed by Peter Bridgewater

Typeset by DP Photosetting, Aylesbury, Bucks
Colour separations by Fotographics, Hong Kong

AUTHOR'S ACKNOWLEDGEMENTS
Special thanks are due to the following for their help in
preparing the book: Fiona Campbell, Graeme
Carmichael, Eldridge Pope & Co, Gees Wines Ltd, Sheila
Halley, Donald Kenwrick-Cox, Margaret Pigott of
Harvey's Wine Museum, Matthew Quirk, Catherine Scott,
Vinceremos Wines, and Robin Yapp.

PUBLISHER'S ACKNOWLEDGEMENTS
The Publisher would like to thank the following individuals and organisations
for supplying photographs and/or wine labels for inclusion in this book:
Cephas Picture Library/Nigel Blythe: pp 72–3, 150–1;
CPL/R Prynne: p 153; CPL/Mick Rock: pp 2–3, 8, 12–13, 52–3, 98–9, 110–1,
122–3, 138–9; CPL/Roy Stedall: pp 86–7; CPL/Ted Stephan: pp 10–11;
Columbia Winery: p 125; Food and Wine from France: pp 13, 15;
Michael Goff: Endpapers; Lamberhurst Vineyards: p 112;
Cantine Giorgio Lungarotti: p 55; Robert Mondavi: pp 123, 124;
Montana Wines Ltd: pp 139, 140; Pilton Manor: p 111; Raimat Barcelona:
pp 7, 87, 89; Barone Ricasoli: pp 9, 53, 54; Schloss Johannisberg: p 75;
Schloss Vollrads: pp 73, 74; S Smith & Son Ltd: p 141; Ian Sumner:
pp 6, 7, 10, 11; Taylor's Port: pp 99, 100, 101; Wines from Spain: pp 88, 151.

Published simultaneously in the United States of
America by Bulfinch Press, an imprint and
trademark of Little, Brown and Company (Inc.),
in Great Britain by Little, Brown and Company (UK) Ltd
and in Canada by Little, Brown and Company (Canada) Limited.

PRINTED IN SINGAPORE

Title page: Autumn vineyards at Barbaresco in Piedmont, Italy.

Contents

Introduction

THINK OF A GREAT WINE. Château Margaux, say. How do you visualise it? Is it as the poet puts it, a beaker full of the warm South with beaded bubbles winking at the brim? Or is it the elegant symmetry of a colonnaded, neo-classical house, and the proud legend *Premier Grand Cru Classé*?

Keats's words are evocative, of course, but there's really no getting away from the fact that a famous wine is irresistibly associated with its label. Great labels, indeed, are more familiar to countless wine lovers than the wines themselves – for few of us have the chance to drink the classic wines of the world on anything other than the most special of occasions.

Collectable classics from Bordeaux and Burgundy.
═ • ═

And once the revered bottle has been drained to its last, we are left only with the memory – and the label. It is to wine lovers who wish to remember those special bottles that this book is dedicated, giving pride of place to the labels and an opportunity to record impressions of the wine.

From the collector's point of view, the classic wine labels are a source of fascination in their own right. Many are quite beautiful, and in recent times producers all over the world have brought the 'designer' element into labelling as they strive to compete for prominence on merchants' shelves.

It was not always so. In the long history of winemaking, the paper label has played a comparatively brief part, and it was not until this century that producer-labelled wines were shipped in any significant quantity to major markets such as Britain and the United States. This is simply because wines were always exported in cask. Even when glass bottles came into use in the 17th century they functioned purely as decanters. Glassware was then very much more valuable than wine.

By the beginning of the 19th century, the cylindrical bottle was ushering in the era of 'vintage' wines – the product of a single harvest from an individual estate which could be bottled, sealed with a driven cork and stacked in a suitable cellar. In these early days, the wines were invariably bottled by the shipper, so those that were labelled would carry the merchant's colours rather than those of the producer.

The first paper labels employed on a large scale by the winemakers themselves were probably those on château-bottlings made by the major Bordeaux estates from the 1850s. Even then, only a fraction of each vintage would be thus bottled – the bulk going in cask to merchants in Bordeaux or abroad until château-bottling became the norm from the early 1900s.

Labels have never been a wholly reliable

guarantee of wine's authenticity. It is one of the simplest frauds to relabel a cheap wine with the livery of a very much grander one. As long ago as 1855, the year of the celebrated classification of Bordeaux's top wines, two thousand

The author extending his own collection.

═ • ═

cases of ordinary claret put up for auction locally included a good few masquerading as the *premier des premiers*, Château Lafite.

Before producer-bottling, a common practice was for the winemaker to supply stamped and dated corks to merchants buying by the cask, rationing the corks to the quantity appropriate to the volume of wine purchased. Sealed under a lead capsule, this made for a very much more secure guarantee of origin than a mere paper label.

Today, even though virtually all the world's fine wines are bottled at source, corks and capsules still fulfil that function. Labels from every producing country still proclaim proudly that wines are bottled by the maker, even though this has been standard practice worldwide for a generation and more.

Of course much of the wording on wine labels is there by requirement of the law. Strict regulations in the major producing nations call for all manner of information. Importing countries may impose rules too. Britain, for example, has required all wines offered for retail sale to carry a printed descriptive label since as long ago as 1860.

But now the role of the wine label is to allure as well as to inform. The message may be as spare as that of the world's greatest sweet white wine: 'Château d'Yquem – Lur-Saluces – 1986' decorated with nothing more than the Lur-Saluces family heraldic coronet. Or it may be the lengthy dissertation that covers most of the distinctly homely label of Grange Hermitage, widely acknowledged to be Australia's top wine – and certainly its most expensive.

Given the limited scope, the ingenuity of label designers is remarkable. As well as the producers themselves, many retailers commission superb labels for their 'buyer's own brand' wines, contriving to accommodate a considerable amount of vital wording into some stunning images.

An eye-catching label is no guarantee, of course, of a wine that will please. Rather in the way of brilliantly hued insects whose colouring warns predators of the poison in their bodies, a particularly garish label may well herald a wine to be avoided.

When it comes to the classic wines, the role of the label is a more subtle one. An integral part of the enjoyment of a great wine is the

Spanish cava bottle-ageing in style at Raimat.

═ • ═

knowledge that what is in the glass is rated among the finest. The pleasure in drinking Château Margaux 'blind' – anonymously – cannot hope to compare with doing so as part of the full ritual of admiring the label, opening and pouring the wine with due reverence and formulating opinions as to whether it does or does not live up to expectations.

Unfortunately, the best thing about many classic wines can occasionally turn out to be the label itself. Wine merchants are not above offering very poor vintages of famous names to customers who wish purely to 'drink the label'. The craze for collecting the celebrated labels of Château Mouton-Rothschild has brought prices for execrable vintages of that wine, such as 1973 and 1974, up to the levels of very much better years.

Opposite: Torres vines at Catalonia's Riudella castle.

Coveted though some labels are, they are functional items, not made to last. As any enthusiastic collector knows, separating label from bottle and preserving it in good condition can be a challenge.

To begin with it is vital to store wine bottles in a way that protects treasured labels. In a very damp cellar, paper will discolour quickly. Dirt and dust will eventually etch into paper, so if necessary store the bottles labels-down, taking care not to damage the surfaces on the horizontal sections of the rack.

Opening and pouring the wine calls for similar diligence, of course. Decanting is a helpful precaution, or there are various drip-stop devices for use in the bottle's neck to prevent the runnel of wine that can ruin a label.

Removing the label is a delicate operation. As a rule, producers use water-based glues, so soaking the bottle in hot water for an hour or two – or over a longer period if necessary – should do the trick. Stubborn glues may call for boiling water – in which case a metal container should be used (an ice bucket filled with a kettleful of water is ideal).

Unhappily, some winemakers use oil-based adhesives for their labels. Even in boiled water, these substances may not lose their grip. If the label has not floated off within a few hours, try adding a sprinkling of washing powder, as the emulsifying effects of detergents do work on certain adhesives. But don't overdo it, as detergents are abrasive and will damage the label if too concentrated.

Should this fail, it is worth trying to loosen the label at its edge with a long-bladed knife. It's important to ease the blade under the length of the label's edge, as raising the paper by one corner will inevitably cause it to tear.

Sangiovese, the grape at the heart of Chianti.

Some labels, it has to be admitted, simply refuse to unstick and will self-destruct at the first attempt to ease them off with any sort of implement. Champagne and wines from Australia and the United States are frequent offenders. (On a personal note, my own last resort when completely frustrated in an attempt to remove a much-coveted label has been to send the remains of it, along with a pleading letter, to the producer. In most, but not all, cases the ploy has engendered a sympathetic response – and a mint-condition label.)

Once detached from the bottle, carefully rinse the label clean of any residual adhesive. To preserve it in good condition, pat the label dry with a clean glass cloth and press it. The ideal method is to use a flower press, but placing the label between two clean sheets of paper and inserting these in a heavy book – weighted if necessary – will do almost as well. It is vital the label should be damp when it goes into the press.

Leave it for two or three days, and the label should emerge perfectly dry and flat, and ready for adding to the album. For fixing, simply use conventional stamp hinges, one per corner. Never use glue – it makes it impossible to remove the label at a later date, and will rapidly discolour the paper.

Making brief notes about the wine alongside its label will add greatly to the pleasure to be had in the future from leafing through the album's pages. Without a few details written down, even the most unforgettable aromas and flavours can slip the mind. So can the occasion on which the wine was drunk, where it was acquired, and what price was paid.

Each space on the album pages provides a

Drip-stoppers protect labels from ruinous runnels.

═ • ═

simple grid in which to enter these items. The sections devoted to describing the wine itself are divided into separate entries for appearance, nose and taste to make it reasonably straightforward to record the essential characteristics in each case.

On page 158 is a glossary of terms which includes some of those widely used by the professionals to note their impressions of wines. These may be a help in making your own notes, but there is no limit to the vocabulary you can call upon! The point of recording the details is to remind the drinker how the wine performed on the day: Did its colour suggest it was mature enough (too-young red wines tend to look purple)? Was there any of the lychee aroma the experts say you should look for in that Gewürztraminer? Did that Australian red have the oaky flavour its label claimed, or did that 20-year-old claret still have that grip of tannin that suggests years to go before it will begin to fade?

A typical entry might look like this for, say, a good *premier cru* Chablis, around six years old:

APPEARANCE Greeny-gold. Very attractive.
NOSE Fresh, recognisable chardonnay. Hint of vanilla.
TASTE Very dry but with richness, too. Good acidity.
COMMENT A success! Unlike so many pale and thin versions, this Chablis has benefitted from a few years in bottle with richness of colour and flavour but still crisply fresh.

It remains only to wish every owner of this book reasonably consistent good luck with those treasured bottles. May the wines in every case live up to the labels!

France is first for famous names.

= • =

Left: Mustard blooms in California's Inglenook vineyard.

= • =

CHAPTER ONE

France

France is the capital of the world of wine. The labels of the great properties are veritable icons to wine aficionados. And it is to the standards of France's best that winemakers everywhere aspire.

Above: Cabernet sauvignon grapes ripening in Bordeaux.
Left: Pinot noir vines on the Montagne de Reims, Champagne.

= • =

Collecting French Labels

THE DIVERSITY of French wine is awesome, and unrivalled by any other nation. In the Bordeaux region alone, some 20,000 producers are bottling wines under their own labels or those of countless co-operatives. In Burgundy and the valleys of the Loire and Rhône, in Alsace, Champagne and the re-born regions of the Mediterranean South, it is the same story.

Grapes and grandeur at St Emilion.
= • =

Collecting individual wines from this vast firmament is greatly simplified by the systems of classification that so famously categorise the output of the major regions. In a series of such exercises begun in 1855 with the establishment of the Médoc 'top 60' as a marketing device for the Great Exhibition in Paris of that year, Bordeaux has classified several hundred further estates in the Graves, Médoc, St Emilion and Sauternes into variously codified *crus classés*.

In Burgundy, the picture is less clear, although many vineyards have been designated *premier cru* status and thus can be pigeon-holed into neat lists. The problem is that since 1789, when the Church was stripped of its ownership of virtually all the Burgundian vineyards, the tenure of the land has become acceleratingly fragmented. One *premier cru* field may now be split up among a dozen or more separate owners – each desirous of making wine under his own label from his particular few rows of vines. Where this simply is not practicable, the farmer sells his harvest to a *négociant-éleveur* who buys in from several other growers on the site in order to accumulate sufficient wine for an economic bottling under the *cru* label.

What all the regions of France do have in common is the national *appellation d'origine contrôlée* code. The designation guarantees that the wine concerned conforms to a whole raft of local and national rules, and ensures that every label conveys vital descriptive information. Similarly, the lesser codes, *vin délimité de qualité supérieure* and *vin de pays*, are guarantees of the origin and authenticity of the wine.

Sauternes harvesting continues into late autumn's chill.
= • =

Under all three codes, labels must carry the designation itself – *AC* or *AOC*, *VDQS* or *Vin de Pays* – plus the specific appellation or region of origin. The name and location of the bottler (who may or may not be the sole producer) must appear, as must the volume of wine in the bottle – namely 75cl under European Community regulations. Names of the individual estates, vintages and grape varieties are optional, as are

Vines at Hunawihr, Alsace.

— • —

classifications such as *grand cru classé* or that proud but now rather redundant boast *mise en bouteille au château*. Helpful indicators of the style of wine – *brut* for dry champagne, *demi-sec* for sweet whites – are not compulsory.

Between the requirements of the law and the producer's desire to allure and inform, French wine labels can broadly be counted on to be the world's most reliable and lucid. Not that the information displayed on the label can be taken as a guarantee that the drinker will find the contents to his or her taste, of course, but what it reveals should keep costly mistakes to a minimum.

In France more than in any other country, the year in which the wine is made is a crucial factor. The climates of all the major regions are at best capricious, and cannot be counted on to produce crops of consistent quality. When it comes to collecting classic wines, it is vital to choose vintages that represent good value for money. A bad vintage of a *grand cru classé* claret is likely to be a poor deal at anything over half the price of a good one. On the other hand, 'unfashionable' vintages such as Bordeaux 1983 (overshadowed by 1982 and 1985) and 1988 in almost every region (totally upstaged by 1989) can nevertheless be of terrific quality and relatively inexpensive.

For comparative ratings of vintages in France and elsewhere since 1970, see the chart on page 160.

'Great Wine' — GRAND VIN

Commune or parish — CHATEAU **LYNCH ✦ BAGES** — Name of the estate

GRAND CRU CLASSÉ — Classification

Bottled at the property — PAUILLAC — Guarantee of origin

APPELLATION PAUILLAC CONTROLEE

Vintage — 1982 — A CAZES Propriétaire à PAUILLAC (FRANCE) PRODUCE OF FRANCE — 750 ml — Producer

GREAT WINE

The term has no legal force under French law, but *Grand Vin* appears on the label of many Bordeaux wines, usually signifying that this is the premier wine of the estate.

THE ESTATE

As an individual property making wine entirely from its own grape harvest, the *château* can call itself by the estate's name, and depict the house on the label.

COMMUNE

Top-quality wines are identified by their immediate locality, the unique conditions of which play a big part in the wine's character.

CLASSIFICATION

Hundreds of individual estates in Bordeaux – and as many vineyards in Burgundy – are designated *crus classés*, denoting very special quality. This wine is among the Médoc's 60 *Grands Crus Classés*.

BOTTLING

That the wine is bottled at the property rather than shipped in bulk for bottling elsewhere is an assurance of quality. All *cru classé* wine must be château-bottled by law.

GUARANTEE

The commune has its own *appellation contrôlée*, guaranteeing the origin and authenticity of the wine.

VINTAGE

Harvest conditions in France's great vineyards can vary radically, so vintages differ accordingly in quality – and price.

PRODUCER

The name and the address of the producer and/or bottler must appear on all French labels.

CHÂTEAU-MARGAUX
GRAND VIN
MIS EN BOUTEILLE AU CHÂTEAU
1964
PREMIER GRAND CRU CLASSÉ
FRANCE
APPELLATION MARGAUX CONTROLÉE
DÉPOSÉ
Imp. ARCÉ, Bordeaux

Dessin inédit   de César

1967   1967

Cette récolte a produit :
246.590 Bordelaises et ½ B^es de 1 à 246.590
3034 Magnums de M 1 à M 3034
34 Grands Formats de GF 1 à GF 34
double magnums, jéroboams, impériales
3.000 "Réserve du Château" marquées R.C.
Ci. N° 22574

Philippe de Rothschild

Château
Mouton Rothschild

BARON PHILIPPE DE ROTHSCHILD PROPRIÉTAIRE A PAUILLAC
APPELLATION PAUILLAC CONTRÔLÉE
TOUTE LA RÉCOLTE MISE EN BOUTEILLES AU CHÂTEAU

OCCASION	
DATE AND PLACE OF PURCHASE	
APPEARANCE	
NOSE	
TASTE	
COMMENT	
	PRICE

OCCASION	
DATE AND PLACE OF PURCHASE	
APPEARANCE	
NOSE	
TASTE	
COMMENT	
	PRICE

GRAND VIN
DE
CHATEAU LATOUR

PREMIER GRAND CRU CLASSÉ

APPELLATION PAUILLAC CONTRÔLÉE

PAUILLAC-MÉDOC

1962

MIS EN BOUTEILLES AU CHÂTEAU

MARQUE DÉPOSÉE   G. CHARIOL_BORD*

SOCIÉTÉ CIVILE DU VIGNOBLE DE CHÂTEAU LATOUR
PROPRIÉTAIRE A PAUILLAC-GIRONDE

MIS EN BOUTEILLE AU CHÂTEAU

CHATEAU LAFITE-ROTHSCHILD
1985
PAUILLAC
APPELLATION PAUILLAC CONTRÔLÉE

PRODUCE
OF FRANCE   75cl

DEPOSE   SOCIÉTÉ CIVILE DU CHATEAU LAFITE ROTHSCHILD, PROPRIÉTAIRE A PAUILLAC (GIRONDE)

OCCASION	
DATE AND PLACE OF PURCHASE	
APPEARANCE	
NOSE	
TASTE	
COMMENT	
	PRICE

OCCASION	
DATE AND PLACE OF PURCHASE	
APPEARANCE	
NOSE	
TASTE	
COMMENT	
	PRICE

OCCASION	
DATE AND PLACE OF PURCHASE	
APPEARANCE	
NOSE	
TASTE	
COMMENT	
	PRICE

OCCASION	
DATE AND PLACE OF PURCHASE	
APPEARANCE	
NOSE	
TASTE	
COMMENT	
	PRICE

OCCASION	
DATE AND PLACE OF PURCHASE	
APPEARANCE	
NOSE	
TASTE	
COMMENT	
	PRICE

OCCASION	
DATE AND PLACE OF PURCHASE	
APPEARANCE	
NOSE	
TASTE	
COMMENT	
	PRICE

OCCASION	
DATE AND PLACE OF PURCHASE	
APPEARANCE	
NOSE	
TASTE	
COMMENT	
	PRICE

OCCASION	
DATE AND PLACE OF PURCHASE	
APPEARANCE	
NOSE	
TASTE	
COMMENT	
	PRICE

OCCASION	
DATE AND PLACE OF PURCHASE	
APPEARANCE	
NOSE	
TASTE	
COMMENT	
	PRICE

BORDEAUX: MEDOC

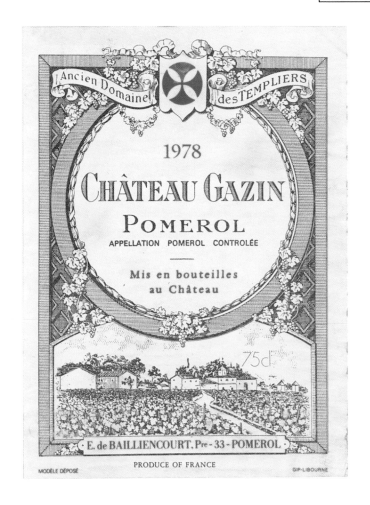

OCCASION	
DATE AND PLACE OF PURCHASE	
APPEARANCE	
NOSE	
TASTE	
COMMENT	
	PRICE

OCCASION	
DATE AND PLACE OF PURCHASE	
APPEARANCE	
NOSE	
TASTE	
COMMENT	
	PRICE

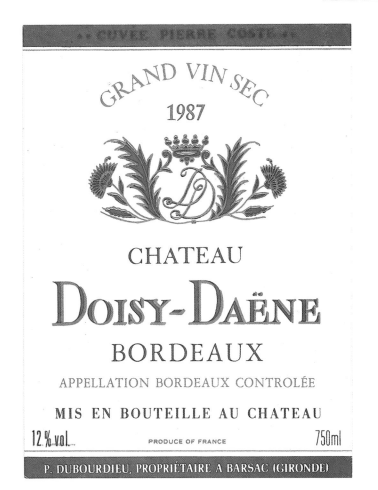

OCCASION	
DATE AND PLACE OF PURCHASE	
APPEARANCE	
NOSE	
TASTE	
COMMENT	
	PRICE

OCCASION	
DATE AND PLACE OF PURCHASE	
APPEARANCE	
NOSE	
TASTE	
COMMENT	
	PRICE

OCCASION	
DATE AND PLACE OF PURCHASE	
APPEARANCE	
NOSE	
TASTE	
COMMENT	
	PRICE

OCCASION	
DATE AND PLACE OF PURCHASE	
APPEARANCE	
NOSE	
TASTE	
COMMENT	
	PRICE

OCCASION	
DATE AND PLACE OF PURCHASE	
APPEARANCE	
NOSE	
TASTE	
COMMENT	
	PRICE

OCCASION	
DATE AND PLACE OF PURCHASE	
APPEARANCE	
NOSE	
TASTE	
COMMENT	
	PRICE

1978

37,5 cl.

CHÂTEAU
LA TOUR BLANCHE

1er
CRU
CLASSÉ

SAUTERNES

Appellation Sauternes Contrôlée

MIS EN BOUTEILLE AU CHATEAU

ÉCOLE DE VITICULTURE ET D'OENOLOGIE
BOMMES (GIRONDE) - FRANCE

DONATION OSIRIS

CHATEAU AUSONE

SAINT•EMILION

APPELLATION SAINT-EMILION CONTRÔLÉE

1957

Vve C. VAUTHIER & J. DUBOIS-CHALLON

PROPRIÉTAIRES A SAINT-ÉMILION (GIRONDE)

MIS EN BOUTEILLES AU CHATEAU

DÉPOSÉ

Olhet GIP - Libourne

OCCASION	
DATE AND PLACE OF PURCHASE	
APPEARANCE	
NOSE	
TASTE	
COMMENT	
	PRICE

OCCASION	
DATE AND PLACE OF PURCHASE	
APPEARANCE	
NOSE	
TASTE	
COMMENT	
	PRICE

OCCASION

DATE AND PLACE OF PURCHASE

APPEARANCE

NOSE

TASTE

COMMENT

PRICE

OCCASION

DATE AND PLACE OF PURCHASE

APPEARANCE

NOSE

TASTE

COMMENT

PRICE

OCCASION	
DATE AND PLACE OF PURCHASE	
APPEARANCE	
NOSE	
TASTE	
COMMENT	
	PRICE

OCCASION	
DATE AND PLACE OF PURCHASE	
APPEARANCE	
NOSE	
TASTE	
COMMENT	
	PRICE

OCCASION	
DATE AND PLACE OF PURCHASE	
APPEARANCE	
NOSE	
TASTE	
COMMENT	
	PRICE

BORDEAUX

OCCASION	
DATE AND PLACE OF PURCHASE	
APPEARANCE	
NOSE	
TASTE	
COMMENT	
	PRICE

OCCASION	
DATE AND PLACE OF PURCHASE	
APPEARANCE	
NOSE	
TASTE	
COMMENT	
	PRICE

Hospices de Beaune
1985
BEAUNE
Appellation Beaune Contrôlée
Cuvée Dames-Hospitalières

❧

Chaque année, le troisième Dimanche de Novembre, a lieu la célèbre vente aux enchères «à la chandelle» des Grands Vins du Domaine des Hospices, constitué tout au long des siècles grâce à de généreuses donations.

Ces grands vins en tonneaux sont pris en charge par les acquéreurs qui ont la délicate mission de les élever et de les mettre en bouteilles.

Sélectionné, élevé et mis en bouteille par
Emile Chandesais à Fontaines, S.-&-L., France
acheteur traditionnel
à la Vente des Vins des Hospices de Beaune

Produit de France   75 cl

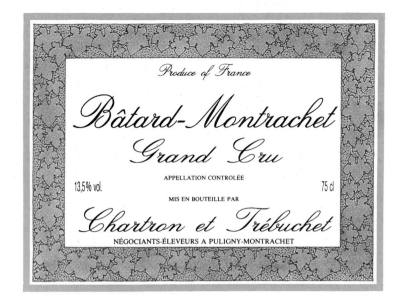

Produce of France

Bâtard-Montrachet
Grand Cru
APPELLATION CONTROLÉE

13,5% vol.   75 cl

MIS EN BOUTEILLE PAR

Chartron et Trébuchet
NÉGOCIANTS-ÉLEVEURS A PULIGNY-MONTRACHET

OCCASION	
DATE AND PLACE OF PURCHASE	
APPEARANCE	
NOSE	
TASTE	
COMMENT	
	PRICE

OCCASION	
DATE AND PLACE OF PURCHASE	
APPEARANCE	
NOSE	
TASTE	
COMMENT	
	PRICE

OCCASION	
DATE AND PLACE OF PURCHASE	
APPEARANCE	
NOSE	
TASTE	
COMMENT	
	PRICE

OCCASION	
DATE AND PLACE OF PURCHASE	
APPEARANCE	
NOSE	
TASTE	
COMMENT	
	PRICE

OCCASION	
DATE AND PLACE OF PURCHASE	
APPEARANCE	
NOSE	
TASTE	
COMMENT	
	PRICE

OCCASION	
DATE AND PLACE OF PURCHASE	
APPEARANCE	
NOSE	
TASTE	
COMMENT	
	PRICE

OCCASION	
DATE AND PLACE OF PURCHASE	
APPEARANCE	
NOSE	
TASTE	
COMMENT	
	PRICE

OCCASION	
DATE AND PLACE OF PURCHASE	
APPEARANCE	
NOSE	
TASTE	
COMMENT	
	PRICE

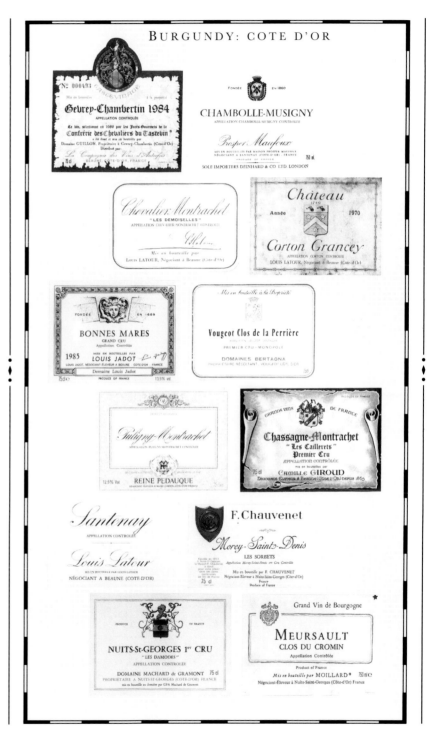

BURGUNDY: COTE D'OR

OCCASION	
DATE AND PLACE OF PURCHASE	
APPEARANCE	
NOSE	
TASTE	
COMMENT	
	PRICE

PRODUIT DE FRANCE

Chablis Premier Cru

VAILLON

APPELLATION CHABLIS PREMIER CRU CONTRÔLÉE

12.8 % VOL.

Mise en bouteilles au

DOMAINE ROBERT VOCORET & SES FILS
PROPRIÉTAIRES-VITICULTEURS A CHABLIS (FRANCE) ℮ 75 cl

VARNIER-SPERNAY

MÉDAILLE
D'OR

PARIS
3 MARS 1990

BEAUJOLAIS
APPELLATION BEAUJOLAIS CONTROLÉE

JEAN GARLON

PROPRIÉTAIRE RÉCOLTANT A 69620 THEIZÉ

12,5 % Vol.   MISE EN BOUTEILLE A LA PROPRIÉTÉ   PRODUIT DE FRANCE   75 cl

OCCASION	
DATE AND PLACE OF PURCHASE	
APPEARANCE	
NOSE	
TASTE	
COMMENT	
	PRICE

OCCASION	
DATE AND PLACE OF PURCHASE	
APPEARANCE	
NOSE	
TASTE	
COMMENT	
	PRICE

OCCASION	
DATE AND PLACE OF PURCHASE	
APPEARANCE	
NOSE	
TASTE	
COMMENT	
	PRICE

OCCASION	
DATE AND PLACE OF PURCHASE	
APPEARANCE	
NOSE	
TASTE	
COMMENT	
	PRICE

OCCASION	
DATE AND PLACE OF PURCHASE	
APPEARANCE	
NOSE	
TASTE	
COMMENT	
	PRICE

OCCASION	
DATE AND PLACE OF PURCHASE	
APPEARANCE	
NOSE	
TASTE	
COMMENT	
	PRICE

OCCASION	
DATE AND PLACE OF PURCHASE	
APPEARANCE	
NOSE	
TASTE	
COMMENT	
	PRICE

BURGUNDY

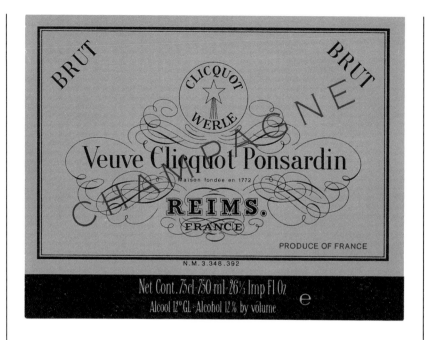

OCCASION	
DATE AND PLACE OF PURCHASE	
APPEARANCE	
NOSE	
TASTE	
COMMENT	
	PRICE

OCCASION	
DATE AND PLACE OF PURCHASE	
APPEARANCE	
NOSE	
TASTE	
COMMENT	
	PRICE

OCCASION	
DATE AND PLACE OF PURCHASE	
APPEARANCE	
NOSE	
TASTE	
COMMENT	
	PRICE

OCCASION	
DATE AND PLACE OF PURCHASE	
APPEARANCE	
NOSE	
TASTE	
COMMENT	
	PRICE

OCCASION	
DATE AND PLACE OF PURCHASE	
APPEARANCE	
NOSE	
TASTE	
COMMENT	
	PRICE

OCCASION	
DATE AND PLACE OF PURCHASE	
APPEARANCE	
NOSE	
TASTE	
COMMENT	
	PRICE

ALSACE AND CHAMPAGNE

OCCASION

DATE AND PLACE OF PURCHASE

APPEARANCE

NOSE

TASTE

COMMENT

PRICE

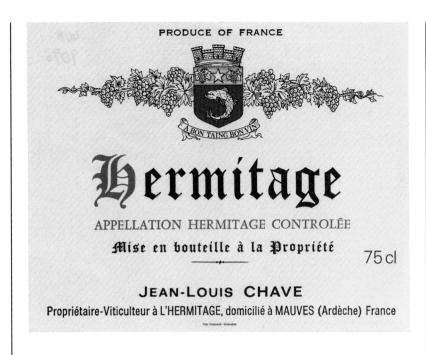

OCCASION	
DATE AND PLACE OF PURCHASE	
APPEARANCE	
NOSE	
TASTE	
COMMENT	
	PRICE

OCCASION	
DATE AND PLACE OF PURCHASE	
APPEARANCE	
NOSE	
TASTE	
COMMENT	
	PRICE

OCCASION	
DATE AND PLACE OF PURCHASE	
APPEARANCE	
NOSE	
TASTE	
COMMENT	
	PRICE

OCCASION	
DATE AND PLACE OF PURCHASE	
APPEARANCE	
NOSE	
TASTE	
COMMENT	
	PRICE

OCCASION	
DATE AND PLACE OF PURCHASE	
APPEARANCE	
NOSE	
TASTE	
COMMENT	
	PRICE

OCCASION	
DATE AND PLACE OF PURCHASE	
APPEARANCE	
NOSE	
TASTE	
COMMENT	
	PRICE

OCCASION	
DATE AND PLACE OF PURCHASE	
APPEARANCE	
NOSE	
TASTE	
COMMENT	
	PRICE

LOIRE AND RHONE

OCCASION	
DATE AND PLACE OF PURCHASE	
APPEARANCE	
NOSE	
TASTE	
COMMENT	
	PRICE

OCCASION	
DATE AND PLACE OF PURCHASE	
APPEARANCE	
NOSE	
TASTE	
COMMENT	
	PRICE

OCCASION	
DATE AND PLACE OF PURCHASE	
APPEARANCE	
NOSE	
TASTE	
COMMENT	
	PRICE

OCCASION	
DATE AND PLACE OF PURCHASE	
APPEARANCE	
NOSE	
TASTE	
COMMENT	
	PRICE

OCCASION	
DATE AND PLACE OF PURCHASE	
APPEARANCE	
NOSE	
TASTE	
COMMENT	
	PRICE

OCCASION	
DATE AND PLACE OF PURCHASE	
APPEARANCE	
NOSE	
TASTE	
COMMENT	
	PRICE

OCCASION	
DATE AND PLACE OF PURCHASE	
APPEARANCE	
NOSE	
TASTE	
COMMENT	
	PRICE

LANGUEDOC AND THE SOUTH

CHAPTER TWO

Italy

Huge production, loose-knit wine laws and an unbridled panache in label design can conspire to make the quest for fine Italian wine a perplexing one. But the great names of Italy still stand among the world's classics.

Above: Fruit ripening for conversion into luscious Tuscan vin santo.
Left: Alpine Lombardy's Valtellina is a rising DOC region.

53

Collecting Italian Labels

THE TWO MILLION vineyards that punctuate Italy from its Alpine valleys to the sub-tropical slopes of Sicily make a quarter of all the wine in the world. Little more than a tenth of this vast output – equivalent to 10 billion bottles a year – is of any defined quality, but amidst it all are some great classic wines.

Italy's wine laws, introduced only as recently as 1963 in an attempt to emulate France's *AC* system, at present do little to guarantee the standards in vineyards and winery they purport to enforce. The basic quality designation *denominazione di origine controllata* (*DOC*) appears on the labels of wines from 230 zones around the country, seemingly regardless of reputation and placing often overgenerous limits on the volume of production.

Brolio castle, near Siena.

So devalued had the *DOC* mark become by the 1980s that the government introduced a new, more stringent rating, *denominazione di origine controllata e garantita* (*DOCG*). This rating is now becoming familiar on the labels of wines from Barbaresco and Barolo in Piedmont, Brunello di Montalcino, Carmignano, Chianti and Vino Nobile di Montepulciano in Tuscany, and Torgiano in Umbria. These are all for red wines. There is just one *DOCG* white wine zone, the obscure Albana di Romagna, but both Frascati and Orvieto are tipped for inclusion shortly.

Other future wine-law changes look like including a new *grand-cru-classé*-style rating for individual estates making the very top wines in each region. To date, the few great single-vineyard wines known outside Italy have enjoyed no distinguishing official quality codification at all.

Casks of Chianti keep cool at Ricasoli.

Quite the opposite is the case for the new-style wines now being so successfully produced by innovators such as Vallana in Piedmont and Antinori in Tuscany. Despite the fact that the Vallana Spanna and Antinori's Tignanello are among Italy's greatest red wines, both rank simply as *vino da tavola* (table wine) because they include grape varieties not approved under the local *DOC* regulations. Ironically, it is wines such as these that are pioneering Italy's *risorgimento* – resurgence – as a serious producer after so many years of overproduction and declining quality.

For wine-lovers anxious to try Italy's best, therefore, labels are not a reliable guide. But many of the labels themselves, it has to be said, are wonderful to behold – especially on Tuscan wines, where the art of the Renaissance is a popular theme in tribute to the region's capital, and cradle of the movement, Florence.

Tuscany is home to one of the best-known of the winemaking consortia which have established themselves in Italy as custodians of local quality. The Chianti Classico zone covers only a fraction of the Chianti *DOCG* and members of the consortium have long had to meet much higher standards than those demanded under the national regulations. Chianti Classico wines that do qualify are thus labelled, and carry the *Gallo Nero* (black cockerel) symbol.

The most dependable guide to the quality of any Italian wine is likely to be the name of the producer – which must, under the *DOC* rules, appear on the label. In the best-known zones, particular winemakers are earning for themselves justifiably brilliant reputations. In the Alto Adige (Alpine Italy) the names include Gaierhof, J. Hofstatter and Alois Lageder. In the Veneto – home of Bardolino and Valpolicella, Bianco di Custoza and Soave – there are Allegrini and Anselmi, Guerreri-Rizzardi, Pieropan, Quintarelli and Tedeschi. In Piedmont, Ascheri, Giacomo Conterno, Gaja and Pio Cesare are among the best Barbaresco and Barolo producers. Tuscany's great names include Antinori, Badia a Coltibuono, Castello Vicchiomaggio, Castello di Volpaia, Selvapiana and Tenuta di Capezzana. Umbria is dominated by the great Torgiano reds of Lungarotti. Emilia-Romagna, fountainhead of that fizzy phenomenon Lambrusco, has a wonderful chardonnay *vino da tavola*, Terre Rosse, made by Enrico Vallania. Bianchi and Garofoli make fine Rosso Conero in the Marches, and Corvo makes the most dependable wines of Sicily.

Local works of art feature on Umbria's famous Lungarotti labels.

═ • ═

AZIENDA AGRICOLA
GUERRIERI-RIZZARDI

Producer

Valpolicella — Denomination

Denominazione di Origine Controllata
V. Q. P. R. D.

Quality — *Classico Superiore* — Origin

Imbottigliato all'origine dal viticoltore
nella sede in Bardolino, Italia — Estate bottled

Not pasteurised 0,750 lt. NON PASTORIZZATO 12 % Vol.

PRODUCER

The Guerrieri-Rizzardi estate. *Azienda agricola* signifies that the maker has his own property, as do other label terms such as *castello* (castle), *fattoria* (farm), *villa* (manor house) or *casa vinicola* (winery).

QUALITY

As an indication of quality in addition to the *DOC* code, many Italian wines are labelled *classico*. This means they are made by a *consorzio* (association) of winemakers with superior vineyards and special quality checks. *Superiore* means a wine aged a little longer, and a degree higher in alcohol.

NOT PASTEURISED

Many Italian producers pasteurise export wine. to stabilize it. An 'organic' winemaker, Guerrieri is a pioneer of a growing movement towards more natural viniculture.

DENOMINATION

Italy's wines are almost all known by their district of origin, which usually takes its name from a town or village.

ORIGIN

Some 230 zones of Italy are covered by the *DOC* system. The designation on the label means the wine is made from specified grape varieties grown in a defined area, cultivated and vinified by approved means. The VQPRD, *Vin de qualité produit en régions determinées*, is a European Community quality guarantee.

ESTATE BOTTLED

This means bottled at the source by the cultivator. Under *DOC* rules, the place of bottling, and the bottler's name and address, must be stated.

BORGOGNO

Barolo

DENOMINAZIONE D'ORIGINE CONTROLLATA
Produce of Italy

PRODOTTO IMBOTTIGLIATO IN ZONA D'ORIGINE DA

Giacomo Borgogno & Figli

Italia **BAROLO** *Piemonte*

Servire con delicatezza ed alla temperatura di 20-22 C°

e 750 ml · 13,5% VOL.

450/CN

DEPOSITATA

Spanna
del Piemonte
Vino da tavola

Casa fondata
nel 1894

Imbottigliato da
Ditta Agostino Brugo & C.
Romagnano Sesia - Italia
produce of Italy

12% VOL.

750 ML

OCCASION	
DATE AND PLACE OF PURCHASE	
APPEARANCE	
NOSE	
TASTE	
COMMENT	
	PRICE

OCCASION	
DATE AND PLACE OF PURCHASE	
APPEARANCE	
NOSE	
TASTE	
COMMENT	
	PRICE

OCCASION	
DATE AND PLACE OF PURCHASE	
APPEARANCE	
NOSE	
TASTE	
COMMENT	
	PRICE

OCCASION	
DATE AND PLACE OF PURCHASE	
APPEARANCE	
NOSE	
TASTE	
COMMENT	
	PRICE

RECIOTO DELLA VALPOLICELLA

AMARONE

1981

DENOMINAZIONE DI ORIGINE CONTROLLATA
CLASSICO SUPERIORE
PRODOTTO E MESSO IN BOTTIGLIA DALL'AZIENDA AGRICOLA
ALLEGRINI · FUMANE DI VALPOLICELLA · ITALIA

Allegrini

750 ML. e   15% VOL.

Pinot Grigio
Ruländer
Valdadige

DENOMINAZIONE DI ORIGINE CONTROLLATA
IMBOTTIGLIATO DALLA
S.Margherita

S. MARGHERITA S.p.A.   I- FOSSALTA DI PORTOGRUARO
12% VOL.   ITALIA

75 cl. e

OCCASION	
DATE AND PLACE OF PURCHASE	
APPEARANCE	
NOSE	
TASTE	
COMMENT	
	PRICE

OCCASION	
DATE AND PLACE OF PURCHASE	
APPEARANCE	
NOSE	
TASTE	
COMMENT	
	PRICE

OCCASION	
DATE AND PLACE OF PURCHASE	
APPEARANCE	
NOSE	
TASTE	
COMMENT	
	PRICE

OCCASION	
DATE AND PLACE OF PURCHASE	
APPEARANCE	
NOSE	
TASTE	
COMMENT	
	PRICE

OCCASION

DATE AND PLACE OF PURCHASE

APPEARANCE

NOSE

TASTE

COMMENT

PRICE

OCCASION

DATE AND PLACE OF PURCHASE

APPEARANCE

NOSE

TASTE

COMMENT

PRICE

OCCASION	
DATE AND PLACE OF PURCHASE	
APPEARANCE	
NOSE	
TASTE	
COMMENT	
	PRICE

OCCASION	
DATE AND PLACE OF PURCHASE	
APPEARANCE	
NOSE	
TASTE	
COMMENT	
	PRICE

THE NORTH

OCCASION	
DATE AND PLACE OF PURCHASE	
APPEARANCE	
NOSE	
TASTE	
COMMENT	
	PRICE

TIGNANELLO

Vino prodotto con uve sangiovese e, in piccola parte, cabernet in un antico podere di proprietà Antinori sito nella frazione di Mercatale Val di Pesa, e imbottigliato nelle proprie Cantine dai Marchesi Lodovico e Piero

Antinori di Firenze viticultori dal 1385 e fornitori brevettati delle case Reali d'Italia e di Svezia, di S.A. il Duca d'Aosta e della Santa Sede.

1986

ANTINORI

750 ml ℮

IMBOTTIGLIATO IN SAN CASCIANO V.P. (382 FI) DA
MARCHESI L. e P. ANTINORI S.p.A. - FIRENZE - ITALIA

ITALIA
12,5 % vol.

VINO DA TAVOLA DI TOSCANA

IMBOTTIGLIATO ALL'ORIGINE
NELLE CANTINE DI

DALLA C.V.B. RICASOLI S.p.A.
GAIOLE IN CHIANTI

BROLIO
CHIANTI CLASSICO
DENOMINAZIONE DI ORIGINE CONTROLLATA

CASA VINICOLA BARONE RICASOLI
FIRENZE - ITALIA

12,3 % vol.   litri 0,750

OCCASION	
DATE AND PLACE OF PURCHASE	
APPEARANCE	
NOSE	
TASTE	
COMMENT	
	PRICE

OCCASION	
DATE AND PLACE OF PURCHASE	
APPEARANCE	
NOSE	
TASTE	
COMMENT	
	PRICE

COPERTINO

DENOMINAZIONE DI ORIGINE CONTROLLATA

1987 RISERVA

ESTATE BOTTLED

BY

CANTINA SOCIALE COOPERATIVA

COPERTINO

Produce of Italy

e 75 cl.   13% vol.

tenuta di
Capezzana

1985

GHIAIE DELLA FURBA®

VINO DA TAVOLA TOSCANO IMBOTTIGLIATO DAL VITICOLTORE

CONTE CONTINI BONACOSSI

CARMIGNANO · ITALIA · R.I 315/FI

75cl. e   BOTTIGLIA   № 08823   di 15.543   13%vol.

OCCASION	
DATE AND PLACE OF PURCHASE	
APPEARANCE	
NOSE	
TASTE	
COMMENT	
	PRICE

OCCASION	
DATE AND PLACE OF PURCHASE	
APPEARANCE	
NOSE	
TASTE	
COMMENT	
	PRICE

OCCASION	
DATE AND PLACE OF PURCHASE	
APPEARANCE	
NOSE	
TASTE	
COMMENT	
	PRICE

OCCASION	
DATE AND PLACE OF PURCHASE	
APPEARANCE	
NOSE	
TASTE	
COMMENT	
	PRICE

OCCASION	
DATE AND PLACE OF PURCHASE	
APPEARANCE	
NOSE	
TASTE	
COMMENT	
	PRICE

OCCASION	
DATE AND PLACE OF PURCHASE	
APPEARANCE	
NOSE	
TASTE	
COMMENT	
	PRICE

OCCASION	
DATE AND PLACE OF PURCHASE	
APPEARANCE	
NOSE	
TASTE	
COMMENT	
	PRICE

OCCASION	
DATE AND PLACE OF PURCHASE	
APPEARANCE	
NOSE	
TASTE	
COMMENT	
	PRICE

OCCASION	
DATE AND PLACE OF PURCHASE	
APPEARANCE	
NOSE	
TASTE	
COMMENT	
	PRICE

OCCASION	
DATE AND PLACE OF PURCHASE	
APPEARANCE	
NOSE	
TASTE	
COMMENT	
	PRICE

OCCASION	
DATE AND PLACE OF PURCHASE	
APPEARANCE	
NOSE	
TASTE	
COMMENT	
	PRICE

OCCASION	
DATE AND PLACE OF PURCHASE	
APPEARANCE	
NOSE	
TASTE	
COMMENT	
	PRICE

OCCASION	
DATE AND PLACE OF PURCHASE	
APPEARANCE	
NOSE	
TASTE	
COMMENT	
	PRICE

OCCASION	
DATE AND PLACE OF PURCHASE	
APPEARANCE	
NOSE	
TASTE	
COMMENT	
	PRICE

OCCASION	
DATE AND PLACE OF PURCHASE	
APPEARANCE	
NOSE	
TASTE	
COMMENT	
	PRICE

THE CENTRE AND SOUTH

CHAPTER THREE

Germany

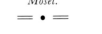 *Rightly famed for the elegance and beauty of its classic white wines, Germany does not, unfortunately, produce correspondingly appreciable labels. To get acquainted with the wines, a knowledge of German label language is vital.*

Above: Late harvest in the Rheingau.
Left: Winter vines at Zeltingen in the Mosel.

Collecting German Labels

IT IS TEMPTING to say that the best approach to appreciating the great wines of Germany is to do so by numbers. The output of the vineyards that extend along the river valleys from Bonn to the Swiss border 200 miles south must be the most precisely defined and regulated grape harvest of any vine-growing nation.

Under wine-law reforms enacted in 1971, the quality wine (*Qualitätswein*) of Germany

Schloss Vollrads is famed for dry riesling wines.

must derive from 11 specified regions (*Anbaugebiete*). Between them, these regions include 35 districts (*Bereiche*) which are divided into 152 vineyard groupings (*Grosslagen*). Thus, a familiar label name such as Piesporter Michelsberg from the Mosel is made up of the district name, Piesport, the vineyard grouping of Michelsberg and general heading of Mosel-Saar-Ruwer as the specified region.

In the quest for Germany's greatest wines,

however, it is necessary to look further. That is, among the 2,600 single vineyards (*Einzellagen*) that can be named on labels instead of the very much less selective vineyard grouping name such as Michelsberg or the notorious Gutes Domthal in the Nierstein district.

Examples of the greatest vineyards are the Schlossböckelheimer Kupfergrube in the Nahe region, the Niersteiner Brudersberg in the Rheinhessen region and the Bernkasteler Doctor in the Mosel. The problem is that the law does not differentiate, through the terms used on labels, between vineyard groupings and individual sites. Yet another good reason for keeping the labels from well-liked bottles as a reminder of the best names!

Where the name of Germany's noblest grape variety, the Riesling, appears on the label it means that this comprises at least 85 per cent of the total. This is a good sign, as virtually all the great white wines of the country are made from this variety. The other widely grown variety is the müller-thurgau, the mainstay of Germany's vast production of ordinary 'medium' wine, but it is never named on labels.

What is not so simple to sum up is the system by which Germany classifies its top-quality wines in terms of taste. When the grapes ripen to a point at which the natural sugar level can be measured on a scale known as the Oechsle, the wine made from them can be labelled with a higher classification, *Qualitätswein mit Prädikat* (*QmP*) – which broadly means quality wine with special

The castle at Vollrads dates from the 14th century.

*Schloss
Johannisberg wines
mature in wood in
cool cellars.*

══ • ══

character. According to the sugar levels reached on the Oechsle scale, *QmP* wines are bracketed into six grades, rising in sweetness, intensity of flavour – and price. These are: Kabinett, Spätlese, Auslese, Beerenauslese, Eiswein and Trockenbeerenauslese.

The first three may not be at all sweet as made wines, as many producers now ferment the must until most or all of the natural sugar turns to alcohol to make a semi-dry (*halbtrocken*) or dry (*trocken*) wine. The last three, all made from grapes that have reached progressively more advanced states of 'noble rot' (*edelfäule*) before picking, will be intensely sweet – and divinely delicious. These latter wines are only made in tiny quantities, and in very few vintages. They have tremendous potential for ageing, transforming over decades into coppery-gold nectar of unique richness.

The success of Liebfraumilch – which is virtually unobtainable in Germany – has overshadowed the greater achievements of the Rhine and Mosel winemakers. Germany has a great deal more to offer, and efforts made to seek out the classic wines will be rewarded.

ESTATE BOTTLED

Erzeugerabfüllung (not usually translated as here) is a useful mark of quality.

REGION

Germany's wine country is divided up into 11 overall regions. Quality wines must state their particular region of origin, in this case the Mosel.

GRAPE

Germany's noblest variety, the Riesling, makes virtually all the country's best wines. Avoid wines that *don't* say Riesling!

CLASSIFICATION

The *QmP* designation applies only to wines made from grapes reaching a specified level of ripeness. The AP (*Amtliche Prüfungsnummer*) code fully identifies the wine's source.

PRODUCER

The name of a winemaker with a good reputation is an important reassurance of quality.

VINTAGE

Harvest conditions vary considerably from year to year, so vintages differ significantly.

DISTRICT

Bernkastel is the *Bereich*, or district, as defined under the law and, likewise, Badstube is the *Grosslage* or grouping of vineyards. This form of description pinpoints all Germany's quality wines to their place of origin.

QUALITY

Kabinett indicates a wine from Germany's *QmP* – top quality – classification. *Kabinett* wines are typically quite dry.

OCCASION	
DATE AND PLACE OF PURCHASE	
APPEARANCE	
NOSE	
TASTE	
COMMENT	
	PRICE

OCCASION	
DATE AND PLACE OF PURCHASE	
APPEARANCE	
NOSE	
TASTE	
COMMENT	
	PRICE

OCCASION	
DATE AND PLACE OF PURCHASE	
APPEARANCE	
NOSE	
TASTE	
COMMENT	
	PRICE

OCCASION	
DATE AND PLACE OF PURCHASE	
APPEARANCE	
NOSE	
TASTE	
COMMENT	
	PRICE

OCCASION	
DATE AND PLACE OF PURCHASE	
APPEARANCE	
NOSE	
TASTE	
COMMENT	
	PRICE

OCCASION	
DATE AND PLACE OF PURCHASE	
APPEARANCE	
NOSE	
TASTE	
COMMENT	
	PRICE

OCCASION	
DATE AND PLACE OF PURCHASE	
APPEARANCE	
NOSE	
TASTE	
COMMENT	
	PRICE

OCCASION	
DATE AND PLACE OF PURCHASE	
APPEARANCE	
NOSE	
TASTE	
COMMENT	
	PRICE

OCCASION	
DATE AND PLACE OF PURCHASE	
APPEARANCE	
NOSE	
TASTE	
COMMENT	
	PRICE

OCCASION	
DATE AND PLACE OF PURCHASE	
APPEARANCE	
NOSE	
TASTE	
COMMENT	
	PRICE

RHINE

OCCASION	
DATE AND PLACE OF PURCHASE	
APPEARANCE	
NOSE	
TASTE	
COMMENT	
	PRICE

MOSEL–SAAR–RUWER

Carl Reh

7.0% vol

A. P. Nr. 3 529 149 222 90

75 d℮

1989
LEIWENER KLOSTERGARTEN
RIESLING KABINETT
QUALITÄTSWEIN MIT PRÄDIKAT

Abfüller: Weinkellerei Carl Reh GmbH & Co. KG, D-5501 Leiwen
Produce of Germany

QR151901

PRODUCE OF GERMANY

MOSEL-SAAR-RUWER

1983er
Serriger Heiligenborn
Riesling
SPÄTLESE

Qualitätswein mit Prädikat
A. P. Nr. 3 561 107 035 84

7,5 % vol   Erzeugerabfüllung   750 ml ℮

Staatsweingut mit Staatlichen Weinbaudomänen
der Landes-, Lehr- und Versuchsanstalt für
Landwirtschaft, Weinbau und Gartenbau (LLVA),
D-5500 Trier

OCCASION	
DATE AND PLACE OF PURCHASE	
APPEARANCE	
NOSE	
TASTE	
COMMENT	
	PRICE

OCCASION	
DATE AND PLACE OF PURCHASE	
APPEARANCE	
NOSE	
TASTE	
COMMENT	
	PRICE

OCCASION	
DATE AND PLACE OF PURCHASE	
APPEARANCE	
NOSE	
TASTE	
COMMENT	
	PRICE

OCCASION	
DATE AND PLACE OF PURCHASE	
APPEARANCE	
NOSE	
TASTE	
COMMENT	
	PRICE

OCCASION	
DATE AND PLACE OF PURCHASE	
APPEARANCE	
NOSE	
TASTE	
COMMENT	
	PRICE

OCCASION	
DATE AND PLACE OF PURCHASE	
APPEARANCE	
NOSE	
TASTE	
COMMENT	
	PRICE

MOSEL

OCCASION	
DATE AND PLACE OF PURCHASE	
APPEARANCE	
NOSE	
TASTE	
COMMENT	
	PRICE

CHAPTER FOUR

Spain

From the sherry that was the world's favourite wine five centuries ago to the exciting 'cava' sparkling wines of today, Spain encompasses every style of wine. Its classic wines can rival the best from anywhere.

Above: Deep cellars in the Penedes region.
Left: Valdepeñas lies in the heart of La Mancha's romantic windmill country.

═ • ═

87

Collecting Spanish Labels

SPANISH-BOTTLED quality wine is still a relative novelty in major importing countries such as the UK and the United States. Until 20 years ago, almost the entire export production was shipped in cask and tanker for bottling at the destination. Very often, the 'buyer's own brand' labels would cheerfully declare the contents to be Spanish Burgundy, Spanish Chablis or – the true nadir – Spanish Sauternes.

Today, such wines are mercifully extinct, killed off by tough European Community regulations, and unmourned by Spain's growing army of skilled winemakers – who are understandably anxious to compete with their Mediterranean neighbours in the worldwide market for wines of true quality. The country now has its own equivalent of France's *AC* system, the *Denominacion de Origen*, governing approved zones of production (there are 31 throughout the country) and practices in vineyard and winery.

Sherry is the historic wine of Spain, grown in the cauldron of Andalucia, and spanning an extraordinary range of styles from bone-dry, sea-breeze-fresh young *fino* to succulent, midnight-dark *oloroso*, aged in ancient *solera* casks for decades. Unhappily, the contrived 'pale' and 'medium' sherries with which shippers have tried to entice drinkers in recent times have given even

The bodegas of Valencia produce more wine than any other region of Spain.

= • =

the great classic wines a bad name. So look out for bargain-priced gems from the shippers still making authentic dry sherries – among them Gonzalez Byass, Hidalgo, Lustau, Sandeman and Valdespino.

Among table wines, Rioja claims prominence for its silky, long-aged reds. These are among the few fine wines of the world to be held back in bottle until they are fully mature and ready to drink. *Reserva* wine cannot by law be sold until it is three years old, and *Gran Reserva* must wait five years.

As Rioja's reputation has grown, and its prices with it, the neighbouring Navarra region is emerging from the shadows to produce not just similar, oaky reds at competitive prices, but some innovative wines based on classic French varieties – particularly cabernet sauvignon – as well as the local noble grape, the tempranillo.

Another region making its name is Valdepeñas (it means Valley of the Stones) a *Denominacion de Origen* within the vast plain of

Samples for tasting and blending at a large co-operative.

= • =

La Mancha south of Madrid. The soft red wines made here are more and more commonly aged in oak casks to produce a richer, rounder style that belies the very low prices.

Yet another new name now appearing on Spanish labels is that of Toro, a recently established *DO* close to the north-east tip of Portugal. The wines are big, rich reds, again very inexpensive. Toro's neighbour, Ribera del Duero, is better known, but its classic reds are by no means cheap. Vega Sicilia, the local star, is as costly as a Bordeaux first growth, and indeed includes classic Bordeaux grape varieties in its blend, alongside the ubiquitous local tempranillo.

Perhaps the most famous labels from Spain are those of the Torres family business, in Catalonia's Penedes region. Torres's top red wine, Gran Coronas Black Label, has on more than one occasion been chosen by experts in 'blind' tastings as a better wine by comparison with a whole raft of Bordeaux's finest. Torres also makes some of Spain's crispest, freshest dry white wines (a rare commodity in Iberia) including the worldwide favourite Viña Sol.

Catalonia is also home to Spain's booming sparkling-wine industry. Here they call it *cava* – and local lore has it that this dependably drinkable wine was being made in the region long before that rather better-established sparkler, champagne, had popped its first cork. *Cava*, made by what is known as the Champagne method, has recently come to rival its French counterpart more closely, with the inclusion of locally-grown chardonnay grapes (a major Champagne variety) in the blend. Major *cava* names to look out for include Codorniu, Mont Marcal and Raimat.

Raimat castle's insignia of 'raim' (Catalan for grapes) and 'mat' (hand).
══ • ══

Gran Reserva
Name
Classification
Vintage
Producer
Estate bottled

GRAN RESERVA

Spain's best wines are matured for many years before going on sale. In Rioja a *Gran Reserva* red must age in oak cask and then in bottle for at least five years altogether. *Reserva* wines have at least three years' ageing.

NAME

Few Spanish wines take their names from individual properties. This is a brand name – and a famous one.

CLASSIFICATION

The stamps of Spain's regulating authorities confirm that the wines are made to the standards set under the local *Denominacion de Origen*. This is the emblem of the Rioja *Consejo Regulador* and authenticates the wine. Unfortunately, many producers of *Denominacion de Origen* wines neglect to carry the correct wording on the label – which undermines the scheme's value.

VINTAGE

Even in the heat of Spain, vintages do vary. *Gran Reserva* wines can only be made in good years.

PRODUCER

Bodegas Riojanas is the name of the producer (included by law), in this case one of the Rioja region's major firms, founded in 1890 and with headquarters at Cenicero in the prime winemaking district the Rioja Alta.

ESTATE BOTTLED

Embotellado en nuestro Castillo, 'bottled in our castle' is a direct parallel to France's *mis en bouteille au château*. It is not a common term on Spanish labels, and in this case refers jocularly to Bodegas Riojanas' 20th-century winery, which is embellished with an extraordinary mock-medieval castle tower.

OCCASION	
DATE AND PLACE OF PURCHASE	
APPEARANCE	
NOSE	
TASTE	
COMMENT	
	PRICE

OCCASION	
DATE AND PLACE OF PURCHASE	
APPEARANCE	
NOSE	
TASTE	
COMMENT	
	PRICE

OCCASION	
DATE AND PLACE OF PURCHASE	
APPEARANCE	
NOSE	
TASTE	
COMMENT	
	PRICE

OCCASION	
DATE AND PLACE OF PURCHASE	
APPEARANCE	
NOSE	
TASTE	
COMMENT	
	PRICE

OCCASION	
DATE AND PLACE OF PURCHASE	
APPEARANCE	
NOSE	
TASTE	
COMMENT	
	PRICE

OCCASION	
DATE AND PLACE OF PURCHASE	
APPEARANCE	
NOSE	
TASTE	
COMMENT	
	PRICE

OCCASION	
DATE AND PLACE OF PURCHASE	
APPEARANCE	
NOSE	
TASTE	
COMMENT	
	PRICE

OCCASION	
DATE AND PLACE OF PURCHASE	
APPEARANCE	
NOSE	
TASTE	
COMMENT	
	PRICE

OCCASION	
DATE AND PLACE OF PURCHASE	
APPEARANCE	
NOSE	
TASTE	
COMMENT	
	PRICE

OCCASION	
DATE AND PLACE OF PURCHASE	
APPEARANCE	
NOSE	
TASTE	
COMMENT	
	PRICE

OCCASION	
DATE AND PLACE OF PURCHASE	
APPEARANCE	
NOSE	
TASTE	
COMMENT	
	PRICE

OCCASION	
DATE AND PLACE OF PURCHASE	
APPEARANCE	
NOSE	
TASTE	
COMMENT	
	PRICE

OCCASION	
DATE AND PLACE OF PURCHASE	
APPEARANCE	
NOSE	
TASTE	
COMMENT	
	PRICE

OCCASION	
DATE AND PLACE OF PURCHASE	
APPEARANCE	
NOSE	
TASTE	
COMMENT	
	PRICE

OCCASION	
DATE AND PLACE OF PURCHASE	
APPEARANCE	
NOSE	
TASTE	
COMMENT	
	PRICE

CHAPTER FIVE

Portugal

Light 'green' wines and a
world-renowned rosé, plus
the best of after-dinner wines –
all come from Portugal. But
there are other discoveries to be
made, too, behind this country's
less-familiar labels.

Above: Douro harvest destined for Port.
Left: Vineyards at Cheleiros, north-west
of Lisbon.

99

Collecting Portuguese Labels

THE NAMES on the labels of Portugal's great fortified wines remind us that the port trade was a British creation, and largely remains a British business even today. It was in the 18th century that the first true fortified wines were made by the agents or 'factors' of London shippers whose names are among the most familiar in wine: Croft, Warre, Taylor Fladgate Yeatman, Offley Forrester and Sandeman – all were founded before 1800.

The trade is continuing to expand even now as port finds eager markets throughout the world for its diverse styles, particularly 'late-bottled' wines made from one year's harvest, aged four, five or six years in cask then bottled, ready to drink. But it is the classic wines, old tawnies and vintage ports, that maintain the trade's place among the world's best wine-makers. Despite dramatic price rises in the 1980s, demand for vintages – only 'declared' by most shippers in years of very good harvests – has never been higher. Students of labels should note that a true vintage port will state its date simply as 'Vintage 1985'. 'Late-bottled Vintage', 'Vintage Character' and 'Crusted' ports are not the same at all.

Likewise, beware 'Tawny' port of unstated age, as it has probably been made simply by blending ruby and white ports. True tawnies begin life as fine ruby, gradually fading to a natural tawny colour through years of ageing in casks. These superb wines are sold under authorised labels dated 10, 20, 30 and even 40 years old.

In the lodges at Taylors, Vila Nova de Gaia.

Portugal's other world-famous wine comes from the port country's neighbouring region, the Minho. *Vinho verde* could hardly be in starker contrast to the great fortified wine. Literally 'green wine' it is so-known because the grapes are picked while still immature, to produce aridly dry, sharply acidic flavours to match Portugal's oily cuisine. Most exported *vinho verde* is in fact slightly sweetened to suit more northern tastes.

It is from the Minho that one of the most famous branded wines originates – Mateus Rosé. Launched in the 1950s under the name of the Mateus palace depicted on the label (a building entirely unconnected with the wine) this is the ultimate 'market-oriented' product. Mateus is made to different sweetnesses according to its destination, and even the sparkle is optional: Britain is accustomed to the slightly fizzy version; America knows Mateus only as a still pink wine.

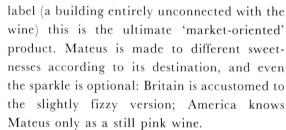

Douro terraces descend precipitously into the river.

The classic table wines of Portugal derive from the Bairrada and Dão immediately south of the port country's Douro valley, and further south in the regions surrounding Lisbon, particularly Alentejo, Ribatejo and Setubal. Bairrada reds can be very long-lived, maintaining their dark colour as the rich, hefty fruit becomes round and smooth over ten years in bottle. *Reserva* wines (theoretically made only from exceptional harvests) from Caves São João are highly rated. The grandest wines of the Dão, meanwhile, are labelled *garrafeira*, signifying the best vintages and at least three years ageing in cask and bottle before release.

These powerful, very dry red wines are often criticised as old-fashioned in style – but no one would say they lack distinction. Best names for reds (the white wines are very much less interesting) are Alianca, Caves Velhas, Dom Ferraz, Grão Vasco and Caves São João again.

Alentejo is the province covering most of southern Portugal, and the source of many fine red wines which, at this present time of reform (not to mention confusion) for the nation's wine laws, lack legal definition. Individual names to seek out are Tinto da Anfora from the João Pires winery (in Setubal), and the Tinto Velho wines made on J.M. da Fonseca's Rosado Fernandes estate and by the Adega Cooperativa de Redondo.

Ribatejo is known for its *garrafeira* reds, especially the Romeira and Caves Velhas brands and those from Carvalho, Ribeiro & Ferreira. Setubal, once so well-known for its now unfashionable sweet Moscatel, is today much more renowned for its state-of-the-art João Pires winery, producing a superb grapey-dry white Muscat, and some fine single *quinta* (estate) reds such as the cabernet sauvignon-based Quinta da Bacalhoa and the beaujolais-like Quinta da Santo Amaro. No less impressive are the wines from Setubal's other great *adega* (winery) – the Quinta de Camarate reds and whites of Jose Maria da Fonseca.

Last word must go to Portugal's great island wine, Madeira. These smoky, fortified wines range from the driest style, Sercial through the richer Verdelho and sweet Bual to the super-luscious Malmsey – in each case the style taking its name from the constituent grape variety. At ten or more years old these can be very special wines indeed.

'Cesto vindimo' baskets, traditional for Douro harvesting.

═ • ═

The wine

Style

Estate

VINHO VERDE

REGIÃO DEMARCADA
BRANCO

Region

SOLAR DAS BOUÇAS

ENGARRAFADO NA ORIGEM
SOLAR DAS BOUÇAS - SOCIEDADE VITIVINICOLA, S.A.
PROZELO

10,5 % Alc. by Vol. **AMARES**
PRODUCT OF PORTUGAL

750 ML e
75 cl e

Bottler

THE WINE	REGION

As with most Portuguese table wines, it is the type of wine, rather than an individual estate or producer, that dominates the label.

Região Demarcada (RD) means the wine is made in a legally demarcated region, in this case the large tract of the Minho province designated for the production of *vinho verde* ('green' wine – though most of it is, in fact, red). There are a dozen *RD*s in Portugal, and wine-law reforms instituted in 1991 should ultimately raise this number to 26.

STYLE	

Branco means white, and *tinto* red. Lighter red wines are sometimes labelled *clarete*.

ESTATE	BOTTLER

Unusually for a Portuguese wine, this one is made from grapes harvested from a single estate. Thus the name – and the grand house – on the label. The term for an estate is more commonly *quinta*.

Engarrafado na origem means the wine is bottled at its place of origin, the Solar das Boucas estate at the Minho town of Amares. The fact that it is producer-bottled indicates a fine wine above the average in a country where the great majority of wines come from co-operatives.

QUINTA DO
NOVAL
1985
VINTAGE PORT

BOTTLED IN 1987   PRODUCE OF PORTUGAL

This wine is the product of a single vineyard, the famous Quinta do Noval, Pinhão, and is shipped by the proprietors **QUINTA DO NOVAL** *- Vinhos, S. A., Vila Nova de Gaia. It should be allowed to mature in bottle for some years, and carefully handled and decanted a few hours before serving*

RED PORTUGUESE WINE PRODUCED FROM A SINGLE VINEYARD

1985

QUINTA DE
SANTO AMARO

from the Setubal Peninsular

RED TABLE WINE

PINHAL NOVO – PALMELA

Bottled for Joao Pires & Filhos Lda – Pinhal Novo – Palmela

11.5% vol   **PRODUCE OF PORTUGAL**   75cl℮

OCCASION	
DATE AND PLACE OF PURCHASE	
APPEARANCE	
NOSE	
TASTE	
COMMENT	
	PRICE

OCCASION	
DATE AND PLACE OF PURCHASE	
APPEARANCE	
NOSE	
TASTE	
COMMENT	
	PRICE

OCCASION	
DATE AND PLACE OF PURCHASE	
APPEARANCE	
NOSE	
TASTE	
COMMENT	
	PRICE

OCCASION	
DATE AND PLACE OF PURCHASE	
APPEARANCE	
NOSE	
TASTE	
COMMENT	
	PRICE

OCCASION	
DATE AND PLACE OF PURCHASE	
APPEARANCE	
NOSE	
TASTE	
COMMENT	
	PRICE

OCCASION	
DATE AND PLACE OF PURCHASE	
APPEARANCE	
NOSE	
TASTE	
COMMENT	
	PRICE

11% alc./vol.　　VINHO TINTO　　℮　75 cl
VIN ROUGE - RED WINE

PRODUZIDO E ENGARRAFADO POR JOÃO PIRES & FILHOS, LDA. - PINHAL NOVO
A PARTIR DE UVAS DA QUINTA DA BACALHÔA PROPRIEDADE DE THOMAS E CATHRYN SCOVILLE

PRODUCT OF PORTUGAL-PRODUIT DU PORTUGAL

OCCASION	
DATE AND PLACE OF PURCHASE	
APPEARANCE	
NOSE	
TASTE	
COMMENT	
	PRICE

OCCASION	
DATE AND PLACE OF PURCHASE	
APPEARANCE	
NOSE	
TASTE	
COMMENT	
	PRICE

OCCASION	
DATE AND PLACE OF PURCHASE	
APPEARANCE	
NOSE	
TASTE	
COMMENT	
	PRICE

OCCASION	
DATE AND PLACE OF PURCHASE	
APPEARANCE	
NOSE	
TASTE	
COMMENT	
	PRICE

OCCASION	
DATE AND PLACE OF PURCHASE	
APPEARANCE	
NOSE	
TASTE	
COMMENT	
	PRICE

OCCASION	
DATE AND PLACE OF PURCHASE	
APPEARANCE	
NOSE	
TASTE	
COMMENT	
	PRICE

OCCASION	
DATE AND PLACE OF PURCHASE	
APPEARANCE	
NOSE	
TASTE	
COMMENT	
	PRICE

OCCASION	
DATE AND PLACE OF PURCHASE	
APPEARANCE	
NOSE	
TASTE	
COMMENT	
	PRICE

OCCASION	
DATE AND PLACE OF PURCHASE	
APPEARANCE	
NOSE	
TASTE	
COMMENT	
	PRICE

CHAPTER SIX

The Rest of Europe

Austria and Greece, the new free-market economies of the East and, weather-permitting, England all have their place on Europe's winemaking map.

Above: Ripening grapes at Pilton Manor, Somerset.
Left: Bird-netted vines at Breaky Bottom, Sussex.

Collecting Labels from the Rest of Europe

THE DRAMATIC changes in European political and economic fortunes that have taken place in the last thirty-or-so years have done much to re-shape the continental wine trade and its business with the world outside. Membership of the European Community, extended now to Greece, Portugal and Spain as well as original partners France, Germany and Italy, means new standards of production enforced in virtually all the major vineyards of western Europe.

Eastern European winemakers have long been acknowledged as potential competitors in

Cask sampling at Lamberhurst, Kent.

the world market, and now their new-found freedom promises a veritable flood from Bulgaria, Hungary, Rumania, even Czechoslovakia.

Bulgaria's ubiquitous Suhindol Cabernet Sauvignon is already the biggest-selling brand of red wine in Britain – appropriately partnering Yugoslavia's rather less-exciting Laski Rizling, the top-selling white brand.

Classic wines from Bulgaria and elsewhere from the fringes are already making their names. Hungary's Tokay is a legendary dessert wine, as are Austria's bargain-priced *Trockenbeerenauslesen*. Greece's Retsina is unique, and its sweet muscats from Samos can be superb.

England, too, in spite of the international notoriety of its climate, has shown signs in recent years that fine English wine is a real possibility. Vineyards such as Biddenden and Chiddingstone in Kent, Chalkhill in Wiltshire and Three Choirs in Gloucestershire are making wines (all white) in an exciting range of styles that certainly compete well for quality with their French and German counterparts.

Label law in England is still in its infancy, not yet subject to anything resembling France's *AC* system. What is firmly established already is that only wine made from English-grown grapes may call itself English Wine. 'Wine' labelled 'British' is an entirely different thing. Such 'tonics', 'sherry' and the like are confected from grape concentrates made in Italy, Cyprus (or farther afield) to which water and yeast are added, just as in home winemaking.

Harvesting at Lamberhurst – between downpours.

WOOTTON

19 90

THE GRAPE STEALERS
Reproduced from 13th century carving in Wells Cathedral

Seyval

DRY
ENGLISH TABLE WINE

10.5%
Vol.

Estate grown and bottled at Wootton Vineyard
North Wootton, Wells, Somerset, United Kingdom

75cl.℮

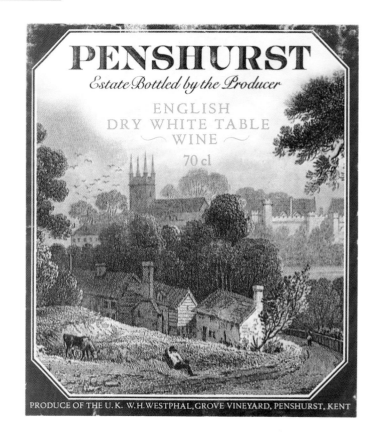

PENSHURST

Estate Bottled by the Producer

ENGLISH
DRY WHITE TABLE
WINE
70 cl

PRODUCE OF THE U.K. W.H.WESTPHAL, GROVE VINEYARD, PENSHURST, KENT

OCCASION	
DATE AND PLACE OF PURCHASE	
APPEARANCE	
NOSE	
TASTE	
COMMENT	
	PRICE

OCCASION	
DATE AND PLACE OF PURCHASE	
APPEARANCE	
NOSE	
TASTE	
COMMENT	
	PRICE

OCCASION	
DATE AND PLACE OF PURCHASE	
APPEARANCE	
NOSE	
TASTE	
COMMENT	
	PRICE

OCCASION	
DATE AND PLACE OF PURCHASE	
APPEARANCE	
NOSE	
TASTE	
COMMENT	
	PRICE

OCCASION	
DATE AND PLACE OF PURCHASE	
APPEARANCE	
NOSE	
TASTE	
COMMENT	
	PRICE

OCCASION	
DATE AND PLACE OF PURCHASE	
APPEARANCE	
NOSE	
TASTE	
COMMENT	
	PRICE

ENGLAND AND WALES

OCCASION	
DATE AND PLACE OF PURCHASE	
APPEARANCE	
NOSE	
TASTE	
COMMENT	
	PRICE

BOUVIER
Trockenbeerenauslese
Apetlon — Neusiedler See
1983
süß   sweet

PRODUCED AND BOTTLED IN AUSTRIA
WEINGUT KELLEREI MOORHOF, ALEX UNGER
7062 ST. MARGARETHEN, BURGENLAND

e 375 ML   ÖSTERREICHISCHER QUALITÄTSWEIN MIT
STAATLICHER PRÜFNUMMER E 1164489 E   11.6%

OCCASION	
DATE AND PLACE OF PURCHASE	
APPEARANCE	
NOSE	
TASTE	
COMMENT	
	PRICE

OCCASION	
DATE AND PLACE OF PURCHASE	
APPEARANCE	
NOSE	
TASTE	
COMMENT	
	PRICE

OCCASION	
DATE AND PLACE OF PURCHASE	
APPEARANCE	
NOSE	
TASTE	
COMMENT	
	PRICE

OCCASION	
DATE AND PLACE OF PURCHASE	
APPEARANCE	
NOSE	
TASTE	
COMMENT	
	PRICE

11,5% Vol.   e 70 cl

WHITE TABLE WINE

RETSINA

TRADITIONAL APPELLATION

PRODUCED AND BOTTLED BY

ACHAÏA-CLAUSS WINE C°

PATRAS - GREECE

PRODUCE OF GREECE

Imported By
WINES OF GREECE LTD.
12. Brick Street LONDON W1

1988
Ersekhalom-Bischofsberger
Blauer Spätburgunder

Ausbruch

töppedt szölöböl készült bor
Product of
Hungary

alc.
11,0% vol

T7678-4

ABFÜLLER:
FERDINAND PIEROTH GMBH
BURG LAYEN/DEUTSCHLAND

Net Contents
750 ml

36128/89

OCCASION	
DATE AND PLACE OF PURCHASE	
APPEARANCE	
NOSE	
TASTE	
COMMENT	
	PRICE

OCCASION	
DATE AND PLACE OF PURCHASE	
APPEARANCE	
NOSE	
TASTE	
COMMENT	
	PRICE

OCCASION	
DATE AND PLACE OF PURCHASE	
APPEARANCE	
NOSE	
TASTE	
COMMENT	
	PRICE

OCCASION	
DATE AND PLACE OF PURCHASE	
APPEARANCE	
NOSE	
TASTE	
COMMENT	
	PRICE

THE REST OF EUROPE

OCCASION	
DATE AND PLACE OF PURCHASE	
APPEARANCE	
NOSE	
TASTE	
COMMENT	
	PRICE

CHAPTER SEVEN

The Americas

Most of the famous names
in American winemaking
were unknown 25 years ago.
Today, the labels of Clos du
Bois, Mondavi and Stag's Leap
are unmistakable not just at
home but around the world.

*Above: American wines are named with
the constituent variety of grape.
Left: The Madonna vineyard at
Carneros, California.*

= • =

123
~

Collecting American Labels

ON AMERICAN WINE LABELS, the first name to look for is that of the grape variety. Throughout the United States and Latin America, wines are made on what is called the 'varietal' basis. Just about every wine is one variation or another on the theme of the chosen species of fruit.

And what a variety there is! In California – which alone makes more wine than Portugal and ranks as the world's sixth largest producer – some 600 wineries are coming up with wines to beat the world. The celebrated Reserve Cabernet Sauvignon wines of Robert Mondavi are compared favourably with the top wines of Bordeaux, and meanwhile the mass-produced cabernets of the world's biggest winemaker, E & J Gallo, are proving equally convincing competition in the branded-wine market

Venerable vines at the Mondavi estate, Napa valley.

against the likes of Mouton Cadet, not just in the US but in Europe.

That other great Bordeaux variety, the merlot, is appearing on the labels of more and more fine Californian wines from makers such as Firestone, Inglenook and Sterling. The classic varieties of Burgundy, pinot noir and chardonnay are also widely planted, making red and white wines at every level. Mondavi, Saintsbury and Trefethen are among the best for pinot noir. Good names for chardonnay include Clos du Bois, Fetzer and Jekel.

California and its winemaking heartland the Napa Valley do not entirely dominate fine winemaking in the United States. Among other producing states, Washington in the Pacific northwest is the strongest contender for classic wines, with the Columbia and Kiona wineries to the fore. New York State, Oregon and Texas are also in the running, and even Canada has a nascent wine business based on vineyards in Ontario.

The Napa is sheltered by wooded hills.

United States wine law took a new turn in 1980 with the introduction of Approved Viticultural Areas. New AVAs are continually being added and to date there are about 100 throughout the USA. Ultimately, the AVAs will be comparable to France's *AC*s, defining not just the geographical district as they do now, but identifying practices in the vineyard and winery and establishing 'typicity' as only *AC*s do. In the meantime, the loose State and County regulations rarely call for any information to be displayed on labels.

A quirk of US law that does show up in print is the legislation that allows American winemakers to label their sparkling wines 'Champagne', red wines 'Burgundy', 'Claret' and 'Chianti' and white wines 'Chablis' and 'Moselle'. Producers in Europe are understandably infuriated, although this has not prevented several leading French and German firms from buying major Californian wineries.

Foreign ownership is a large factor in the recent success of Latin American wines, mainly from Chile and, to a lesser extent, Argentina. The Spanish family firm of Torres is making excellent cabernet sauvignon reds and chardonnay and sauvignon dry whites in Chile's Curico district, and the American-owned Santa Rita winery in the Maipo valley has a classic Cabernet Reserve of exceptional quality. Other Chilean wineries to watch are Jose Canepa, Cousino Macul and Los Vascos.

Argentina produces even more wine than the United States, most of it for domestic consumption, but big foreign-owned wineries such as Bodegas Bianchi are now moving into export-quality wines. Smaller concerns have lately

Winter cultivation in Washington State's Columbia vineyards.

been winning important prizes in European wine fairs – usually an indispensable aid to finding overseas distribution. Labels to look out for include those of Bodegas Canale, Finca Flichman and Roblevina.

Region

Estate bottled

Vintage

Variety

Producer
Alcohol

ESTATE BOTTLED

Only properties within an AVA may use the term estate bottled.

VINTAGE

Single-vintage American wines can include up to five per cent of wine from other years.

PRODUCER

The maker's name and address must appear on all labels.

ALCOHOL

In other producing countries, alcohol levels are indicated on labels for information. In the US, this item also serves as a warning, lately supplemented with official advice that drinking the wine 'may cause health problems'.

REGION

Napa Valley has been an Approved Viticultural Area since 1981 – one of the first declared. It is not obligatory for the initials AVA or the full term to appear on labels, and this is inevitably diminishing the public impact of the scheme. So far more than 100 AVAs have been established in California and elsewhere in the US.

VARIETY

Californian wines labelled with the name of a grape variety – as virtually all of them are – must be composed of at least three-quarters of the variety stated. The name of the variety, stated alongside its place of origin, tells the drinker much of what the wine should taste like – taking its character from the known elements in the fruit and the soil.

BELVEDERE

DISCOVERY SERIES

RED TABLE WINE

1983 SONOMA COUNTY

1984
Napa Valley
CHARDONNAY
ALCOHOL 13.5% BY VOLUME

PRODUCED AND BOTTLED BY
ROBERT MONDAVI WINERY
OAKVILLE, CALIFORNIA

OCCASION	
DATE AND PLACE OF PURCHASE	
APPEARANCE	
NOSE	
TASTE	
COMMENT	
	PRICE

OCCASION	
DATE AND PLACE OF PURCHASE	
APPEARANCE	
NOSE	
TASTE	
COMMENT	
	PRICE

OCCASION	
DATE AND PLACE OF PURCHASE	
APPEARANCE	
NOSE	
TASTE	
COMMENT	
	PRICE

OCCASION	
DATE AND PLACE OF PURCHASE	
APPEARANCE	
NOSE	
TASTE	
COMMENT	
	PRICE

OCCASION	
DATE AND PLACE OF PURCHASE	
APPEARANCE	
NOSE	
TASTE	
COMMENT	
	PRICE

OCCASION	
DATE AND PLACE OF PURCHASE	
APPEARANCE	
NOSE	
TASTE	
COMMENT	
	PRICE

OCCASION	
DATE AND PLACE OF PURCHASE	
APPEARANCE	
NOSE	
TASTE	
COMMENT	
	PRICE

OCCASION	
DATE AND PLACE OF PURCHASE	
APPEARANCE	
NOSE	
TASTE	
COMMENT	
	PRICE

1987 WASHINGTON STATE
CABERNET SAUVIGNON

PRODUCED & BOTTLED BY STATON HILLS VINEYARD & WINERY
WAPATO, WA U.S.A.   BW-WA 109   ALCOHOL 12.5% BY VOL.

1986
ESTATE BOTTLED

Yakima Valley

CABERNET SAUVIGNON

PRODUCED   AND   BOTTLED   BY   KIONA   VINEYARDS   WINERY
BW-WA-73 WEST RICHLAND, WASHINGTON, ALCOHOL 12.5% BY VOLUME

OCCASION	
DATE AND PLACE OF PURCHASE	
APPEARANCE	
NOSE	
TASTE	
COMMENT	
	PRICE

OCCASION	
DATE AND PLACE OF PURCHASE	
APPEARANCE	
NOSE	
TASTE	
COMMENT	
	PRICE

OCCASION	
DATE AND PLACE OF PURCHASE	
APPEARANCE	
NOSE	
TASTE	
COMMENT	
	PRICE

OCCASION	
DATE AND PLACE OF PURCHASE	
APPEARANCE	
NOSE	
TASTE	
COMMENT	
	PRICE

OCCASION	
DATE AND PLACE OF PURCHASE	
APPEARANCE	
NOSE	
TASTE	
COMMENT	
	PRICE

OCCASION	
DATE AND PLACE OF PURCHASE	
APPEARANCE	
NOSE	
TASTE	
COMMENT	
	PRICE

OCCASION	
DATE AND PLACE OF PURCHASE	
APPEARANCE	
NOSE	
TASTE	
COMMENT	
	PRICE

NORTH AMERICA

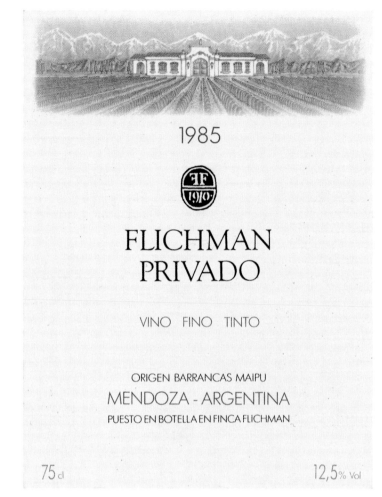

OCCASION	
DATE AND PLACE OF PURCHASE	
APPEARANCE	
NOSE	
TASTE	
COMMENT	
	PRICE

OCCASION	
DATE AND PLACE OF PURCHASE	
APPEARANCE	
NOSE	
TASTE	
COMMENT	
	PRICE

OCCASION	
DATE AND PLACE OF PURCHASE	
APPEARANCE	
NOSE	
TASTE	
COMMENT	
	PRICE

OCCASION	
DATE AND PLACE OF PURCHASE	
APPEARANCE	
NOSE	
TASTE	
COMMENT	
	PRICE

OCCASION	
DATE AND PLACE OF PURCHASE	
APPEARANCE	
NOSE	
TASTE	
COMMENT	
	PRICE

OCCASION	
DATE AND PLACE OF PURCHASE	
APPEARANCE	
NOSE	
TASTE	
COMMENT	
	PRICE

SOUTH AMERICA

OCCASION	
DATE AND PLACE OF PURCHASE	
APPEARANCE	
NOSE	
TASTE	
COMMENT	
	PRICE

CHAPTER EIGHT

Australia & New Zealand

 These brave new winemakers have burst into the world market with the lack of ceremony that typifies their outlook. But many of the wines have already earned their place among the classics.

Above: High-rise cask-ageing at the Montana winery.
Left: The undulating slopes of the Coldstream Hills Vineyards, Victoria.

═ • ═

Collecting Labels from Australia and New Zealand

 THERE WAS A TIME, barely a generation back, when the best Australian labels bore names like Kanga Rouge and Koala Burgundy – because they were the funniest. Fine Australian wine was a contradiction in terms, a standing joke.

Not any more. Equipped with the latest technology and possessed of weather patterns and terrains that can match the most ideal in France, Australia's new generation of young winemakers is producing wines that are competing with Europe's best very seriously indeed. Enterprises such as Brown Brothers, Penfolds and the Rosemount Estate have become household names in Britain and the United States, with wines to compete at all quality levels, and at keen prices.

The key has been Australia's adoption of the classic French grape varieties, and the decision to make the wines on a 'varietal' basis. Just as they do in California, producers throughout Australia – and New Zealand – primarily identify their wines by the variety.

Australian labels, though not yet governed by any state or national regulations that could be compared to the European systems, are among the most clear and instructive of any in the world (with the added advantage, admittedly, that they are written in English!). The grape variety stated can be assumed to comprise 100 per cent of the wine. Even where two varieties are blended, it is common for the label to declare, for example, 60% Cabernet/ 40% Shiraz. For enthusiasts, there is often a feast of details of how the wine was made and matured and over what period, and even tasting notes as a guide to what to expect.

Vines grow in every state, with the prime region, South Australia, accounting for more than half the national crop. The vineyards here lie inland from Adelaide, encompassing several great names – Barossa Valley, Coonawarra, McLaren Vale, Padthaway and Riverland. Winemakers in the region have familiar-sounding names, too – Hardy's, Orlando, Penfolds (makers of Australia's premier red wine, Grange Hermitage, and owners of the great Magill Estate on Adelaide's edge), Tolleys, and Wynns.

The Montana homestead, Marlborough.
═ • ═

Harvest time at Marlborough.
═ • ═

Western Australia is a comparatively small player – just five per cent of the total – but its Margaret River district produces some of the country's finest. The winery best known abroad is Houghton – for a good varietal range.

New South Wales is also dominated by the reputation of one region, the Hunter Valley, 100 miles north of Sydney. Here the wineries to watch include Rosemount in the white-wine specialising Upper Hunter and, in the Lower, the Evans Family's Rothbury Estate, Lake's Folly, Lindeman and Tyrrell.

The hinterland of Melbourne is home to the vineyards of Victoria State. The region is most famously associated with the dessert wines of Brown Brothers – whose labels are instantly recognisable. But dry whites and some very successful reds are being made in new vineyards such as Great Western (for sparkling wines), Milawa, Murray River and Rutherglen. Top winemakers include Chateau Tahbilk, Mildara, Taltarni and Tisdall.

New Zealand's rise into the firmament of fine-wine producing countries has, if anything, been even more meteoric than that of Australia. Not until the 1980s were the first exciting chardonnay and sauvignon whites seen in export markets, but these vibrantly fresh and characterful wines are now internationally known. New Zealand's extraordinary range of micro-climates, created by the country's unique geography, makes just about anything possible. Good red wines from cabernet sauvignon grapes are already appearing. The winery names to seek out on the labels (which are, to date, unregulated by any official appellation system) are Babich, Cloudy Bay, Matua, Montana and Te Mata.

Wine in cask at Samuel Smith's Yalumba winery, South Australia.

Vintage

State

Producer

Bin number

Variety

VINTAGE

The dates on Australian wines need to be taken on trust – in the absence of any national law defining the percentage of wine that must derive from the stated vintage.

STATE

As is often the case, the narrowest definition of the wine's geographical origin is the State – an area twice the size of France! So far, pilot *appellation contrôlée*-type schemes modelled on the French system have not taken hold in Australia.

PRODUCER

Australia's well-known winemakers – and Penfolds is the biggest – have high standards of their own which offer the best guarantee of quality in this least-regulated of producing nations.

BIN NUMBER

'Kalimna Bin 28' is a style of brand name popular with Australian producers. The number implies little more than a wine carefully blended from selected vats, but can nevertheless be taken to indicate a superior product.

VARIETY

The 'varietal' name of the grape used is the first key to identifying Australian wines – though any given variety can assume several different personalities according to where it is planted within the continent. Where the label shows two varietal names (such as cabernet/shiraz) the first one mentioned will have been the larger part of the blend.

ORLANDO

VETUS PURUM

SOUTH EASTERN AUSTRALIA

Cabernet Sauvignon

1985

G. GRAMP & SONS
EST 1847

WINE MADE IN AUSTRALIA 750ML

BOTTLED BY G. GRAMP & SONS PTY. LTD. ROWLAND FLAT S.A. 5352 13.2% ALC./VOL.

IMPORTED BY ORLANDO WINES PTY LTD UK LONDON SW6 1PA

THIS WINE WAS VINTAGED AT OUR ROWLAND FLAT WINERY FROM GRAPES GROWN IN THE LANGHORNE CREEK, KEPPOCH, COONAWARRA AND SOUTHERN VALES DISTRICTS

OCCASION	
DATE AND PLACE OF PURCHASE	
APPEARANCE	
NOSE	
TASTE	
COMMENT	
	PRICE

HARDYS

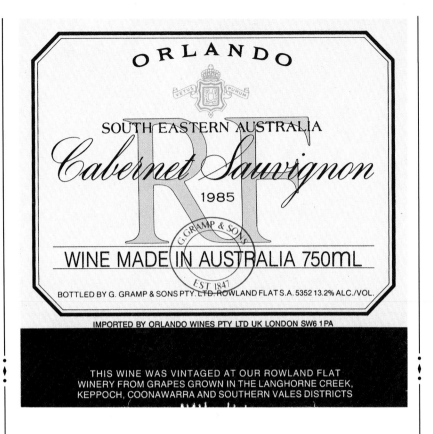

BOTTLED BY THE MAKERS THOMAS HARDY & SONS PTY LTD REYNELL ROAD REYNELLA SA

Jeremy Boot   *Laughing Kookaburra*

1990

CHARDONNAY

SOUTH EASTERN AUSTRALIA

13.0% VOL

WINE MADE IN AUSTRALIA 750 ml

OCCASION	
DATE AND PLACE OF PURCHASE	
APPEARANCE	
NOSE	
TASTE	
COMMENT	
	PRICE

OCCASION	
DATE AND PLACE OF PURCHASE	
APPEARANCE	
NOSE	
TASTE	
COMMENT	
	PRICE

OCCASION	
DATE AND PLACE OF PURCHASE	
APPEARANCE	
NOSE	
TASTE	
COMMENT	
	PRICE

OCCASION	
DATE AND PLACE OF PURCHASE	
APPEARANCE	
NOSE	
TASTE	
COMMENT	
	PRICE

OCCASION	
DATE AND PLACE OF PURCHASE	
APPEARANCE	
NOSE	
TASTE	
COMMENT	
	PRICE

750 ml e

12.5% ALC./VOL.

WYNNS
OVENS VALLEY
NORTH EAST VICTORIA
SHIRAZ
VINTAGE 1984

WINE PRODUCT OF AUSTRALIA

PRODUCED AND BOTTLED BY

WYNN WINEGROWERS PTY LTD MELBOURNE

IMPORTED BY HATCH, MANSFIELD & COMPANY LIMITED,
ST. JAMES'S LONDON SWIY 6AU.

BROWN BROTHERS

Chardonnay

LIMITED PRODUCTION

PRODUCED & BOTTLED AT MILAWA BY BROWN BROTHERS.

MILAWA VINEYARD PTY LTD MILAWA VICTORIA.

Milawa Estate

SPECIAL LIMITED PRODUCTION

Distinctive varietal wines and selected quality binnings, which highlight style and flavoursome characteristics, are bottled separately. Due to the small production, they are available only in limited quantities.

ALCOHOL 11.5% BY VOLUME
WINE MADE IN AUSTRALIA 750 ml

OCCASION	
DATE AND PLACE OF PURCHASE	
APPEARANCE	
NOSE	
TASTE	
COMMENT	
	PRICE

OCCASION	
DATE AND PLACE OF PURCHASE	
APPEARANCE	
NOSE	
TASTE	
COMMENT	
	PRICE

OCCASION	
DATE AND PLACE OF PURCHASE	
APPEARANCE	
NOSE	
TASTE	
COMMENT	
	PRICE

OCCASION	
DATE AND PLACE OF PURCHASE	
APPEARANCE	
NOSE	
TASTE	
COMMENT	
	PRICE

OCCASION	
DATE AND PLACE OF PURCHASE	
APPEARANCE	
NOSE	
TASTE	
COMMENT	
	PRICE

OCCASION	
DATE AND PLACE OF PURCHASE	
APPEARANCE	
NOSE	
TASTE	
COMMENT	
	PRICE

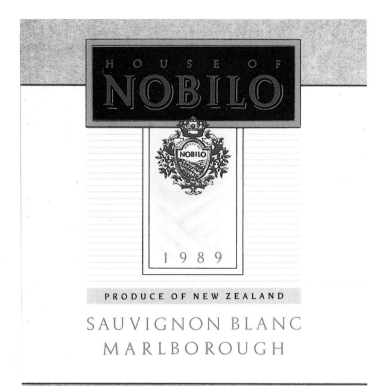

HOUSE OF
NOBILO

1989

PRODUCE OF NEW ZEALAND

SAUVIGNON BLANC
MARLBOROUGH

750 ml.e. | VINTED & BOTTLED BY NOBILO VINTNERS LTD. WINEMAKERS AT HUAPAI | ALC. 12.5% VOL.

EST 1916

NEW ZEALAND
SAUVIGNON BLANC
HAWKE'S BAY
1986

PRODUCED & BOTTLED BY BABICH WINES LTD., HENDERSON, AUCKLAND
PRODUCE OF NEW ZEALAND

Alcohol 12% by volume

750ml

OCCASION	
DATE AND PLACE OF PURCHASE	
APPEARANCE	
NOSE	
TASTE	
COMMENT	
	PRICE

OCCASION	
DATE AND PLACE OF PURCHASE	
APPEARANCE	
NOSE	
TASTE	
COMMENT	
	PRICE

AUSTRALIA AND NEW ZEALAND

OCCASION	
DATE AND PLACE OF PURCHASE	
APPEARANCE	
NOSE	
TASTE	
COMMENT	
	PRICE

CHAPTER NINE

The Rest of the World

Given today's technology and the will to succeed, winemakers can produce drinkable wines almost anywhere. Here are some of the more collectable off-beat wine nations.

Above: Worldwide, primitive winemaking is giving way to quality production – under some exotic labels. Left: Budding vines at Obuse, Nagano Ken, Japan.

Collecting Labels from the Rest of the World

THAT THE word alcohol is given to us from the Arabic language is a constant reminder that the making of wine had its origins in the Middle East. Even today, there are pockets of winemaking activity in the Muslim world: the rump of France's vast vineyard enterprises in Algeria still produces the notorious 'Red Infuriator' and Morocco's Rhône-like 'Tarik' has a following abroad.

But the only true fine wine of the Middle East is from the celebrated vineyard of Château Musar in the Lebanon. Here, the intrepid Franco-Lebanese Serge Hochar grows cabernet sauvigon and cinsaut grapes, and turns them into lush red wines – in the middle of a war zone. If ever there was a label with a story behind it, it is Château Musar.

Israel's modern winemaking tradition dates back to experimental plantings made in the region 100 years ago by the Rothschild family –

Delaire Estate, Stellenbosch, South Africa.
= • =

Paarl is the centre of South Africa's KWV state winemaking concern.
= • =

better known for Château Lafite. Quality wines today are still a rarity, and confined to vineyards planted in the Golan Heights, this time by an American. The wines which have emerged so far into the wider world are a good dry white sauvignon blanc called Yarden, and Gamla, a red from cabernet sauvignon.

Much farther east, India now has its very own 'Champagne-style' wine, made in the hills above Bombay and rejoicing in the name Omar Khayyam. In spite of everything, it is a very good sparkling wine by any standards. Onwards yet, even China is producing its own wines – among which the Tsingtao brand is worth discovering.

It is to the south that the best of the rest lie, in South Africa – where political reforms may or may not allow this important producing nation back on to the world stage.

75 cl.
WINE

ALC. 14% VOL.
PRODUCE OF LEBANON

1982

MARQUE   DÉPOSÉE

Chateau Musar

★

GASTON HOCHAR
PROPRIÉTAIRE VITICULTEUR

IMPORTED BY: CHATEAU MUSAR (UK) LIMITED - LONDON

MISE EN BOUTEILLES AU CHATEAU   GHAZIR - LIBAN

OCCASION	
DATE AND PLACE OF PURCHASE	
APPEARANCE	
NOSE	
TASTE	
COMMENT	
	PRICE

OCCASION	
DATE AND PLACE OF PURCHASE	
APPEARANCE	
NOSE	
TASTE	
COMMENT	
	PRICE

OCCASION	
DATE AND PLACE OF PURCHASE	
APPEARANCE	
NOSE	
TASTE	
COMMENT	
	PRICE

OCCASION	
DATE AND PLACE OF PURCHASE	
APPEARANCE	
NOSE	
TASTE	
COMMENT	
	PRICE

OCCASION	
DATE AND PLACE OF PURCHASE	
APPEARANCE	
NOSE	
TASTE	
COMMENT	
	PRICE

OCCASION	
DATE AND PLACE OF PURCHASE	
APPEARANCE	
NOSE	
TASTE	
COMMENT	
	PRICE

OCCASION	
DATE AND PLACE OF PURCHASE	
APPEARANCE	
NOSE	
TASTE	
COMMENT	
	PRICE

OCCASION	
DATE AND PLACE OF PURCHASE	
APPEARANCE	
NOSE	
TASTE	
COMMENT	
	PRICE

THE REST OF THE WORLD

OCCASION	
DATE AND PLACE OF PURCHASE	
APPEARANCE	
NOSE	
TASTE	
COMMENT	
	PRICE

The Language of the Label

*A BRIEF ROUND-UP of everyday label vocabulary
from around the world plus, to help with
making notes, some of the most widely used
tasting terms (in quotation marks).*

AP On German labels, the *Amtliche Prüfungsnummer* is the key to the wine's authenticity as a *Qualitätswein*. See page 75.

AVA Approved Viticultural Area, eg Napa Valley, on United States labels. See page 125.

ABBOCCATO Italian for medium-dry.

ALCOHOL Content is typically expressed in percentage of volume – from 8 to 14% for table wines; 16 to 21% for fortified wines.

AMABILE Italian for medium-sweet.

AMONTILLADO A style of sherry with a naturally chestnut-gold colour and dry, nutty flavour.

AMOROSO A sweet, dark sherry style.

ANNATA Italian for vintage.

APPELLATION CONTRÔLÉE See page 14.

'APPLEY' Tasting term applied to good, fresh young white wines including those from chardonnay grapes and Mosel rieslings.

'AROMA' The characterising smell of a grape variety, eg the blackcurrant aroma of cabernet sauvignon.

AUSLESE German quality designation. See page 75.

'BALANCE' The decisive element in wine – which should have correct balance between acidity and fruitiness.

BEERENAUSLESE See page 75.

BEREICH See page 75.

BIANCO Italian for white.

BLANC DE BLANCS White wine – usually champagne – made from white grapes.

BLANCO Spanish for white.

BLUSH Palely pink wine, often labelled as 'white', made from black-skinned grapes.

BODEGA Spanish for a wine cellar, wine shop or even winemaking establishment.

'BODY' The weight and density of a wine, as a full-bodied red.

BRANCO Portuguese for white.

BRUT Very dry sparkling wine.

BUAL A sweet style of Madeira. See page 101.

CAVA Spanish sparkling wine. See page 89.

CÉPAGE French for vine. A wine labelled 'Cépage Syrah' is thus made from syrah grapes.

CLASSICO Superior Italian wine. See page 55.

COSECHA Spanish for harvest or vintage.

CÔTE French for slope or hillside. The 'côtes' wines of a region are often claimed to be the best as hillside vineyards produce better fruit than those on the flat.

CRÉMANT 'Creaming' sparkling wines have a less forceful fizz than traditional *mousseux* types such as champagne.

CRIANZA 'Nursery' in Spanish applies to wines aged at least two years before release.

CRU 'Growth' is the magic word in ranking France's great wines. See page 14.

CUVE, CUVÉE The French term for vat is widely used on labels to indicate carefully selected wine – from this or that particular vat.

'DEEP' Taster's term for a colour, smell or flavour in wine that has complexity and interest.

DEMI-SEC French for 'half-dry' but often means fairly sweet.

DENOMINAZIONE DI ORIGINE CONTROLLATA See page 54.

DOLCE Italian for sweet. Note that Dolcetto is a dry red Italian wine, made from a grape variety of that name.

EISWEIN Rare German wine made, in theory, from grapes harvested so late in the year that they have frozen on the vine. See page 75.

ÉLEVAGE 'Upbringing' in French is the function of a wine producer who blends, matures and bottles new wines from various sources.

EMBOTELLADO DE ORIGEN Spanish for estate-bottled.

'FAT' Fulsomely rich – either of a great white burgundy or a rich Sauternes.

'FINISH' The flavours and smells of the wine after it has been swallowed. Great wines always have a great finish.

FINO The palest, driest sherry.

'FLESHY' Term describing a notably lush or smooth wine.

'FLORAL' Wine with distinctive scent of flowers.

GARRAFEIRA Top-grade Portuguese wine. See page 101.

HALBTROCKEN German for fairly dry.

HERMITAGE The greatest wine of the Rhône and, confusingly, an Australian synonym for the syrah grape – which makes red Hermitage.

KABINETT German quality designation. See page 75.

LATE HARVEST Usually on sweet wines – namely those from grapes picked late in the season when they have become very ripe.

'LEGS' The streaks of wine that run

down a glass after swirling. Legs that cling to the glass indicate a quality wine with staying power.

LIGHT A term used more and more to describe low-alcohol wines.

MADURO Portuguese for mature or ready-to-drink.

MALMSEY The sweetest style of Madeira. See page 101.

MARSALA Dessert wine from Sicily.

MINOSEGI BOR Top quality designation for Hungarian wines.

MOELLEUX Literally, 'marrowy' in French, applying to soft, rich Loire whites of great distinction, eg Vouvray.

MONTILLA Sherry-like wine from southern Spain, but made without spirit-fortification.

MOUSSEUX Sparkling.

MUSCAT Wine from the grape of this name is usually sweet, eg Muscat de Beaumes-de-Venise, but Alsace Muscat is dry.

NÉGOCIANT Wine broker.

OAK Wines aged in oak casks are often thus labelled, especially outside France. The process adds a distinctive style to both red and white wines.

OLOROSO Spanish for fragrant,

and the darkest style of sherry.

ORGANIC The definition varies, but it should mean wines from vineyards and wineries where synthetic materials are minimised.

PALO CORTADO A rare sherry style combining the characteristics of *amontillado* and *oloroso*.

PÉTILLANT Very slightly sparkling.

QUALITÄTSWEIN German quality wine. See page 74.

QUINTA Portuguese for farm or estate.

RECIOTO Italian wine made with a proportion of overripe, semi-dried grapes. Whites and reds of great concentration.

RESERVA Spanish for wines with extra-long ageing.

'RIPE' Wine in ideal condition, suggesting perfectly ripe grapes at harvest time.

RIZLING Label term for wine from the 'Italian' riesling grape – not to be compared with the noble Rhine riesling variety.

ROSADO/ROSATO Spanish/Italian for rosé.

ROSSO Italian for red.

RUBY Red port. See page 100.

SEKT German sparkling wine.

SERCIAL Dry Madeira. See page 101.

SHERRY The great fortified wine of Jerez in Spain. All other 'sherry', eg British, Cyprus, South African, is to be avoided.

SOLERA The sherry ageing-blending system of series of casks.

SPÄTLESE German quality designation. See page 75.

SPUMANTE Italian for sparkling.

SULFITES 'Contains sulfites' appears on American wine labels. Sulphur products are used in vineyard and winery to some degree in almost all wine production, 'organic' included.

SUR LIE 'On the lees' in French, this applies to Muscadet left, unfiltered, on the yeasty detritus of fermentation in the vat until immediately before bottling – with supposed benefits.

'TANNIC' Describes a red wine not yet mellowed for drinking.

TAWNY Port aged in wood casks. See page 100.

TINTO Portuguese full-bodied red wine.

TROCKEN Dry German wine. See page 75.

TROCKENBEERENAUSLESE Top German wine, at the top end of the Oeschsle scale for sweetness. See page 75.

'VANILLA' The creamy smell and texture of wine matured in oak.

'VARIETAL' A wine with marked characteristics associated with a particular variety of grape.

VENDANGE TARDIVE Late harvest. Wines, usually in Alsace, from grapes that have reached an advanced state of ripeness.

VENDEMMIA Spanish for vintage.

VIN DÉLIMITÉ DE QUALITÉ SUPÉRIEURE French code which guarantees a wine's authenticity. See page 14.

VIN DE PAYS French country wine. Some of France's finest wines, made outside the classic regions, have only this humble ranking.

VIN DOUX NATUREL Fortified, super-sweet white wine from southern France.

VINO DA TAVOLA Italy's humblest grade of wine – but one which is appended to many of that country's very best.

WEINGUT German vineyard producing wine under an individual estate name.

'WOODY' Unlike 'oaky', not a word denoting quality. Woody, like corky, indicates a wine that tastes of something other than wine.

Collectable Vintages

THE CONDITIONS prevailing in respective harvests can conspire to make the wines of any estate quite unrecognisable from one vintage to the next. This is particularly true in the great regions of France, where weather conditions are notoriously inconsistent.

These guides to recent vintages are intended to give the overall picture only, ranking each year in comparative terms on a one-to-ten scale – the higher the figure, the better the rating of the vintage.

SPAIN

Good years for red *Reserva* and *Gran Reserva* Rioja wines include 1975, 1978, 1982, 1985 and 1988.

PORTUGAL

Port vintages declared by a significant number of shippers are 1970, 1975, 1977 (the best since 1963), 1980, 1982, 1983, 1985 and 1990.

CALIFORNIA

Vintages here are more consistent than in, say, Bordeaux and Burgundy. Recent rated years for reds are 1980, 1984, 1985 and 1988; for whites 1985, 1987, 1989.

FRANCE

	Médoc & Graves	St Emilion & Pomerol	Sauternes & Barsac	Côte d'Or Red	Côte d'Or White	Rhône Red	Alsace White
	BORDEAUX			BURGUNDY		RHÔNE	ALSACE
1970	9	9	8	7	7	9	7
1971	6	7	8	9	9	9	10
1972	2	2	2	8	9	8	3
1973	4	4	2	5	6	6	7
1974	3	3	1	3	6	5	6
1975	8	8	9	2	5	3	9
1976	7	7	9	9	9	9	10
1977	2	2	2	3	5	6	5
1978	8	8	5	8	8	10	7
1979	8	8	6	5	6	6	7
1980	5	5	4	5	5	7	5
1981	7	8	6	4	4	6	7
1982	10	10	7	4	6	8	7
1983	8	8	10	8	8	9	10
1984	4	4	5	3	5	6	5
1985	9	9	7	8	9	9	10
1986	8	7	10	6	9	7	7
1987	6	6	3	7	6	6	7
1988	8	9	9	9	8	9	8
1989	9	9	10	8	10	9	9
1990	8	9	9	9	10	9	7

ITALY

	Piedmont reds eg Barolo	Tuscan reds eg Chianti
1970	8	9
1971	10	9
1972	0	2
1973	3	4
1974	8	4
1975	3	9
1976	7	3
1977	2	8
1978	8	9
1979	5	7
1980	4	6
1981	3	6
1982	8	6
1983	6	7
1984	4	4
1985	9	9
1986	6	8
1987	6	7
1988	7	8
1989	9	7
1990	9	9

GERMANY

	Rhine/Mosel Rieslings
1970	5
1971	10
1972	4
1973	7
1974	3
1975	10
1976	10
1977	6
1978	6
1979	7
1980	6
1981	7
1982	6
1983	9
1984	5
1985	8
1986	8
1987	7
1988	9
1989	10
1990	10